Dianna Thomas, Ph.D., is a retired police officer after twenty-three years of service. She has already written a book about the true crimes of fatal domestic violence and child abuse cases. She has a master's degree in psychology and another in biblical counseling. She also has a doctorate in religious education as well. When she met Samantha, she knew she had to get her story out to as many women and parents as she could who have or may experience piercingly thorns.

It has always been her goal to educate individuals and parents of the dangers that lurk in their community. She feels that knowledge is power, and the more you are aware of such predators, the more you will neither be a statistic nor have a broken life, which leads to more statistics. Don't make the mistake of thinking you can spot out a sexual predator; you can't from a distance. They could be your close relative who's an undocumented sexual predator. Once you've read this book, she promises that your life as a parent will change. If you are a sexual assault victim, your life will change for the better from this day forward.

This book is dedicated to my one and only child, Joshua Micah Douglas. I've been in love with him ever since I've met him. He's the love of my life and if I could have drawn a son, he couldn't have been more picture-perfect than Josh. God couldn't have given me a more suitable child than him.

– Samantha Douglas

In loving memory of my husband, Michael Ellis Douglas, better known as 'Esquire.'

Dianna Thomas, Ph.D.

A ROSE TRAMPLED

The Samantha Douglas Story

AUSTIN MACAULEY PUBLISHERS™

LONDON • CAMBRIDGE • NEW YORK • SHARJAH

Ordering Information
Quantity sales: Special discounts are available on quantity purchases by corporations, associations, and others. For details, contact the publisher at the address below.

Publisher's Cataloging-in-Publication data
Thomas, Ph.D., Dianna
A Rose Trampled

ISBN 9781645757405 (Paperback)
ISBN 9781645757412 (Hardback)
ISBN 9781645757429 (ePub e-book)

Library of Congress Control Number: 2020918546

www.austinmacauley.com/us

First Published (2021)
Austin Macauley Publishers LLC
40 Wall Street, Floor 33, Suite 33302
New York, NY 10005
USA

mail-usa@austinmacauley.com
+1 (646) 5125767

I must start by thanking my awesome friend Samantha for sharing her life story with me and the world to read. From writing early segments to the end cover was sometimes a struggle getting through, but we've made it to its finish.

Samantha is an overcomer, happy within herself, and loving life the best she knows how. I thank her for her truthfulness, boldness, and I'm very sorry for what she'd gone through as a child.

Table of Contents

Author's Note   11

Introduction   12

Dianna, the Author   13

Chapter 1: The Beginning   15

Chapter 2: Infatuation   24

Chapter 3: Athena's Marriage   31

Chapter 4: Samantha   34

Chapter 5: Behaviors   39

Chapter 6: Incest   43

Chapter 7: Warning Signs   46

Chapter 8: Samantha's Hurt   50

Chapter 9: Samantha Grows Up Early   63

Chapter 10: First Marriage   69

Chapter 11: Undying Love   74

Chapter 12: It's Not Over   95

Chapter 13: The Absent Youth   98

Chapter 14: Forgiveness   104

Chapter 15: Samantha Moves on   109

Chapter 16: Lessons Learned   121

Chapter 17: A Wiser Samantha   125

Chapter 18: Fearful Samantha   135

Chapter 19: The Baby   144

Chapter 20: The Close Relative   147

Chapter 21: The Pit   153

Chapter 22: A Thorn That Stings   164

Chapter 23: Peace   172

Chapter 24: Family   180

Chapter 25: Major Thorns   192

Chapter 26: Coping   198

Conclusion   204

Author's Note

The events that occurred in this book are true and are recounted from the best of Samantha Douglas' memory. Many witnesses and other victims' statements and names may have been changed for privacy reasons. Samantha Douglas endured incestuous abuse by a very *close*, grown *relative*. His defining character, relationship, and name will not be mentioned in this book. Dialogs from the memory are true and word for word of the life of Samantha Douglas and narrated and written by Dianna Thomas.

-S.D. / D.T

Introduction

Roses are a symbol of love and are one of the most celebrated and beautiful flowers ever grown. They also symbolize elegance and gentlewomen. Oftentimes, from a Christian perspective, it can symbolize heaven and harmony in the world.

The name 'rose' is French from Latin *rosa sericea*. Most of their flowers have five petals except the rosa, which only has four. There are over three hundred species of roses and thousands of cultivars.

Roses come in many forms and can be seen as erect shrubs, trailing, climbing, or stems that are often armed with sharp 'prickles' or 'thorns.'

A rose flowering color can also affect its meaning such as:

Red Rose
Can be given as a gift to express affectionate or romantic love

Dark Pink Rose
Is used for cheering up a dear friend or given as gratitude and appreciation for kindness shown

Light Pink Rose
Is a sign of gentleness, respect, praise, and tributes

White Rose
Is a symbol for reverential occasions, as to honor a friend. It is also given for new beginnings, farewell, respect, and hope for tomorrow.

Orange Rose
Is given as a thank you, sent for best wishes, applaud, salute, or saying I love you

Yellow Rose
Is a symbol of warmth, a toast to friends, or to lift someone's spirits. It is also used to present joy, wisdom, and power.

Beware though, the rose's thorns are very hurtful.

Dianna, the Author

The rose's beauty has a downfall as the sharp growths along the stem, though commonly called 'thorns,' are for the most part, prickles and outgrowths of the epidermis known as the outer layer substance of the stem. They are unlike true thorns, which are modified stems. These prickles on the stems are typically sickle-shaped snares that assist the rose in grabbing onto other plants when growing over it.

This flower has a multipurpose lifespan. It is used for perfume, food and drinks, medicine, art and symbolism, pests and diseases, and a floral emblem of the United States. Roses have long been admired for their fragrance and beauty. It has been chronicled that roses were considered religious symbols, in spite of the early middle ages, as they were disfavored upon as a symbol of Roman superfluity and overabundance. The thorns, while troublesome to gardeners, contribute a practical aspiration. They warrant that roses endure the ploys of humans and animals.

Don't let its beauty fool you because there are other symbols that roses are known for as well. The thorns on roses have long been an image of adversity as well as rituals. Abraham Lincoln once said, "We can grumble because rose bushes have thorns, or be joyful because thorn bushes have roses."

Thorns are a symbol of sin, sorrow, and hardships. As the rose and thorn form together, they represent pain and pleasure, just like life itself. The beauty of the flowering rose expresses promise, hope, and new beginnings. Yet, it is contrasted by thorns which mean loss, pain, and tribulations.

Samantha Douglas's life was just like that. She had more thorns in her first few years of life than most will ever have in their lifetime. The roses were present as well, but the thorns overshadowed their beauty. Everyone living will have the roses in their lives, good times, beauty, and happiness.

Everyone will also have thorns as well, the pain, heartaches and sufferings. Once you have read Samantha's story, you'll appreciate the thorns in your own life and probably will seldom complain about its pricking.

In order to appreciate how far Samantha's come, you'll have to take a look at where she's been, her past. Most times, our past dictates our future. For Samantha, she's broken cycles, made new strides, and overcame the thorns and adversities in her life.

Chapter 1
The Beginning

The Origin

In the early 1900s, Shreveport, Louisiana was a little town nestled between Texas and Mississippi. The town became a steamboat commerce that carried mostly cotton and agricultural crops to local markets and goods to the trading centers. Its sister city is Bossier City and is separated between the Red River.

As the town grew, the racial makeup was literally separated between blacks and whites. Everyone seemed comfortable with what they had in terms of possessions for the most part. Even though the whites had the better jobs, the blacks were just grateful for another day.

Shreveport has had a long history of unjust treatment and resistance in all areas of life. The city serves as an unparalleled site in which intersecting narratives around race, ethnicity, social class, opportunity, democracy, and equity have played out over the past several decades. Many black families of this time have settled into acceptance as the way things were back then. They worked hard and did what they could to provide for their families. Greed wasn't even a word to ponder or a way of life in those days. Enough was all they needed and trust that the good Lord would provide just that.

Athena

Moreover, this day was like any other ordinary day in Shreveport. It was the beginning of autumn and the leaves were turning red, yellow, and brown. It was one of many features as leaves were shedding from their deciduous trees. The daylights had become noticeably shorter and the temperatures were cooling down considerably.

On one brisk and beautiful day, two teen black sisters were walking home from school. Athena was the older of the two sisters. She attended Booker T. Washington High School, a predominately all-black high school nestled in the all-African-American neighborhood of Shreveport. She was on the 'Lionette' drill team, a marching unit dance line that performed routine performances in order to cheer the football crowd on.

In 1949, Booker T. Washington, (BTW), was formed because the educational facilities for blacks were reported to have been in such deplorable condition. Enrollments were considered overcrowded at the other high schools in Shreveport, and thus, a new school was on the block, BTW. Now, with smaller classrooms, there was still more work to be done in the African-American school system. All schools in Shreveport during this time were considered separate but equal.

BTW was considered a model school for African-American children and was a representational model school for blacks. It also had a crowning moment for its accommodations, layouts for traditional academics and profession, as it also specialized in industrial and literacy programs.

Booker Taliaferro Washington, better known as Booker T. Washington or BTW, was born in 1856. He was an American author, educator, orator, and advisor to numerous presidents of the United States of America. Blacks struggled in the south by disenfranchisement and the Jim Crow discriminatory laws. Washington assembled a countrywide alliance of middle-class blacks, renowned church leaders, white philanthropists, and politicians with a long-term aspiration of building the community's monetary vigor and achievement by a focus on self-help and education.

Numerous states used his name, Booker T. Washington, all over the country. Even streets are named after him in the black neighborhoods today. It is a simple reminder of the struggles blacks once faced and the gratitude of Booker T. Washington for the work he had done for them. Many ancient blacks have paved the way for African-Americans, but Booker T. Washington is more noted for creating a better educational system for blacks.

In 1960, BTW High School continued to grow with leaps and bounds. Athletics, sporting events and especially football, were a much-needed entertainment for the students and the black communities. The BTW's Marching Band was a show-style band, as blacks loved entertainment. They participated in many parades, competitions, and other activities. To help soften the entertainment, the 'Golden Elegance' and the 'Lionettes' were added to accompany the band as auxiliaries. These were pretty and shapely girls, who were dressed somewhat sparingly, acquiesced alongside of the band. BTW's band continued to grow vastly and is now known as a mini Grambling State University Marching Band.

The 'Lionettes' sometimes carry either one or multiple flags or pom-poms. They may even perform movements that are based in dance and may also have a motion of gymnastics as well. They wear the mighty colors of maroon and white uniforms in honor of their school colors. The school was known as the BTW Fighting Lions.

Sixteen–year-old Athena had long, wavy black hair. She had medium brown skin and had the shape of a Coca-Cola bottle. After Lionette practice one day, she and her younger sister, Claire, better yet, her stepsister, were walking home to their father's house and Athena's stepmom's house. The stepmom really didn't like Athena and Athena was reluctant to go there because she was a hateful and mean lady. While walking, Athena noticed a very, very light-skinned young male as he was cutting lawn in front of a nice and well-kept house.

"Who is dat fine yellow boy?" asked Athena.

"Awe, that ain't nobody but DJ," said her younger stepsister, Claire.

Athena and her stepsister kept walking as she'd tried to be inconspicuous with this young handsome male. He really didn't take notice of Athena because his main focus was on his lawn mowing. Yet, the girls continued on home.

The girls entered their impoverished home as they were met by their stern stepmother, Ms. Jean. Mrs. Jean was a brown-skinned lady and had a heavy hand toward her children, Athena especially. Mrs. Jean was Claire's real mother and Athena's stepmother. Mrs. Jean had married Athena's real father.

"You need to git out of those skimpy clothes and git in dare and wash dem dishes," said her stepmother, speaking to Athena.

"Yes, ma'am," Athena responded.

Athena was a very obedient child, but it didn't stop her stepmother from being stern, almost too unrelenting. Athena had a strict upbringing, to the point of being breathless. Mrs. Jean needed Athena around the house for all the needed chores. It was like Athena was the house-mom instead of her stepdaughter. Mrs. Jean cared for her other children to no end, but not her stepchild Athena.

Athena's Mother Versus Stepmother

One of the most beautiful aspects of life is the relationship and love between a mother and child. Athena normally lived with her mother, Harriet, and step-father, while other times she visited a couple of days a week with her father and stepmom, Mrs. Jean once she'd gotten older. To go through life without a mother's love can be very cruel and difficult for a child. It can easily destroy them for years to come. Athena's stepmother despised Mrs. Harriet, and Mrs. Harriet didn't really care for her either, and this made it hard for Athena.

Athena had always noticed that she was the black sheep of both families. She was the oldest of her mothers' other children. Athena had also noticed that her mother treated her in a mean and hateful way as well. Her real mother, Mrs. Harriet, had never kissed, hugged, or told her she loved her just like her stepmother. Athena had always felt empty inside and longed for love.

The Love of a Mother

The love of a mother goes to extraordinary measures when it comes to her children. Her love is one of the greatest bonds known to the human race.

Dianna

A mother's love will sacrifice her own security. She uses her own home as collateral to fight for her offspring. The love of a mother is intrinsic. When faced with grave hazards, she will stop at nothing – and spare no one – who endangers the lives of her children.

The love of a mother is solemn. 'Rose-tinted lens' gives way to terror, concerns, and doubts for her children's safety because now, their wellbeing is about more than having a good time.

The Seasons of a Mother's Love

The love of a mother pivots her awareness to her little ones and away from her well-known leisurely purists, interests, and amusements that are too highly priced and self-focused.

A mother's love makes time to flow into herself, knowing it's the principal thing she can do for her family.

A mother's love declares I will do that 'huge thing' later because at this moment, I have more crucial work at home.

The love of a mother doesn't use her children as a blame to put off the 'frightening task' she is bellowed to do at that moment.

A Mother's Love Measures Dissimilar Matters to Different Women

A mother's love may mean that she lingers in a difficult marriage when it's desirable for the children because she knows the stability and wellbeing of her children are more impactful than felling butterflies.

A mother's love gives robustness to conquer apprehensiveness of the unknown and leave hastily the family home for the aim of her children's security.

A mother's love spends an immense amount of money each year to give her children the best opportunities and education money can purchase.

If a mother sees her child's spirit shrivel at school, her love bears her home to soldier their inner-self and to educate them in a place of safety and rapport.

A mother's love says I will hold you, upthrust you, and love you, though I am neither equipped nor primed for this calling.

A mother's love conveys to full term only to offer her baby to a select few who'll amplify them in a way she trusts.

A Mother Does the Best to Her Ability

A mother's love provides her baby at her bosom day to day – many times hour to hour – though she hasn't had a complete night's rest in months.

A mother's love understands her child needs for more nutrients and nourishments and sometimes requires more than she has to grant, but she thanks God that sometimes formula is preeminent.

A mother's love cautiously determines ingredients and meals for her children to assist them to grow sturdy and healthy and uplifts their immune system.

A mother's love will most oftentimes enable her to serve canned fruit and processed meals, stabilizing the fret that fresh food would be preferable, but $20 will only go so far.

A Mother's Love Looks Contrasting in Contrasting Places

A mother's love will position her family on a vessel to retreat to a battling country, risking threat in dreaming of finding a safe sanctuary.

A mother's love subdues blameworthiness and resentment as she releases her baby off each morning at the guardianship of daycare. Craving she could do that occupation, rather than the work that attributes a roof over their heads.

The mother's love comforts her when there is hardly sufficient food to feed her children, let alone leftovers.

A mother's love says she will deliver, devote, and revere you, though her government appraises her as being second-class.

A mother's love says I'm not responsible for what other people may think or utter about my decisions. A mother will do what she believes is appropriate for her, even if it isn't well-liked, because 'trendy' only matters in high school.

Athena

Athena never received the deep love of a mother. When Athena's other siblings came into the world and had grown up a little, Athena really noticed that her mother did indeed not love her, as she saw the difference of how her mother would dote on her sibling and not her. Athena wondered what she could have done to realize such treatment because neither her mom nor stepmom cared for her and mistreated her. She would always question herself and lived in a self-pity party world.

There were even times when Athena's mother, Mrs. Harriet, would get angry with Athena constantly, as it seemed that she'd gotten whippings to no end and sometimes for no reason. Athena's punishments and whippings would be very harsh. Yet, when her siblings had gotten into trouble and got whippings, their chastisements would be light, if they'd gotten chastised at all. As a young child, Athena had been slapped in the face, whipped without clothes on with a belt, and tied to a bed and whipped and called all sorts of names by her mother.

Athena's History Lesson

Athena's grandmother and Harriet's mother, MaMou as they'd called her, was a sweet and kind lady. One Easter Sunday, MaMou had invited her entire family over to her house to eat after church. This day was a beautiful and sunny day. All of her children, grandchildren, great-grands, cousins, and friends were either outside or inside, socializing or cooking. The supremes were playing on the radio and everyone was having a great time with laughter and dancing. Some were watching the small television set in the living room area.

MaMou left the fun and had gone to her back bedroom to get her apron she'd washed earlier. She noticed Athena asleep on her bed. Athena was knocked out and undisturbed by the commotion up front. MaMou tried to wake her, but Athena was sleeping very hard. MaMou touched her and moved her to ask if everything was 'okay.' Athena opened her bloodshot red eyes only to close them again.

Soon, Athena's mother, Harriet, came into the room.

"Girl, git yourself outta dat bed and come and do deese dishes," said Mrs. Harriet. MaMou had taken notice of how Harriet was treating Athena. After a while, MaMou intervened.

"Leave dat girl alone. She needs her sleep," said MaMou.

"Mamma, she needs to help out," Mrs. Harriet said.

"Ya'll got plenty of help. Now git out of here," said MaMou.

"Yes, Mam," Mrs. Harriet said as she rolled her eyes back at Athena.

Mrs. Harriet left the room and MaMou turned on her gospel music and took a seat in her old rocking chair. She sat near the bed where Athena was, as though she was protecting her. MaMou turned on her tiny radio as she had listened for a while to keep her occupied.

After about three hours, Athena awoke. She moved very slow and was stretching as she looked around and finally focused on her grandmother, MaMou, sitting in her old rocking chair.

"I better go help in the kitchen," Athena said.

"Dey got enough help, baby," said MaMou. MaMou got up off her rocking chair and began to sit on the bed next to Athena.

"Why you so tired, baby?" asked MaMou.

"I'm the only one working around the house and I have to git the kids ready for school. I'm just tired, MaMou," Athena hesitantly and reluctantly said very seriously.

"I think my mom hates me, MaMou," said Athena.

"Awe naw, she don't hate you, baby," said MaMou.

The two began to talk about why things were the way they were. At this time, Athena learned from her great-grandmother, MaMou, that she had a different father than the rest of her siblings, something she'd not known before. At age sixteen, Athena's mother, Mrs. Harriet, had gotten pregnant out of wedlock. The young man didn't see fit to marry her, which really embarrassed her. He didn't make her an honorable woman by giving her his last name. So, she later stole his last name, Hampton, just to show people that she was honored when she really wasn't. She gave Athena the name of Athena Hampton like her real father. Later, he'd married someone else and had children for Athena's stepmother, Jean.

Athena's grandmother advised her that Mrs. Harriet was jealous of her. Athena vaguely reminisces.

"Athena, didn't I tell you to wash dem dishes?" said Mrs. Harriet.

"Yes, man I was gitting to it," said Athena.

Her mother walked up to her and slapped her across the face. Athena was very hurt and embarrassed as the blood was coming out of her nose.

Mrs. Harriet had taken her frustrations out on poor little Athena by mistreating her constantly. It was like her mother hated Athena, as she'd reminded Mrs. Harriet of the embarrassment her abandoned father had given her. After some time, her mother did get married to a man named R.C. Murray. Her mother then became Mrs. Murray and they had many children, Athena's siblings. Mr. R.C. always noticed the mistreatment of Athena by her mother and he really felt sorry for her. This made Mrs. Harriet Murray really hateful toward Athena and ultimately jealous of her because Mr. Murray treated Athena well, or fair I should say.

"MaMou, does my mother hate me?" asked Athena.

"Naw, she just going through something, baby," MaMou responded.

"Just trust in da Lord, baby. He'll bring you through," said MaMou.

"It don't seem like it," Athena said.

"He will, baby. Just wait on him," MaMou advised.

Chapter 2
Infatuation

Athena's Puppy Love

Soon, another day after 'Lionette' practice, Claire and Athena saw DJ, but he didn't see them. The two continued to walk home to Athena's stepmom's house. He's cutting the lawn again.

"Dare dat cute guy again," said Athena.

"Mh hmm," said Claire.

The girls kept going toward their house, Athena's stepmom that is. Athena knew the drill – wash the dishes, sweep and mop the floors, and take out the trash. Claire, the younger stepsister, had left the house while Athena had gone into the kitchen to wash dishes for her stepmother. Athena was the only one working slavishly, as her other siblings were playing around amongst themselves. Claire sneakily went outside and up the street to where the light-skinned young male was cutting lawn. She approached him in a way that had gotten his attention. He suddenly stopped cutting the lawn and wiped the sweat from his forehead with his arm.

"Hey, DJ," said Claire.

"Hey, little girl," said DJ.

"Guess what?" asked Claire.

"What?" he replied.

"My sister likes you," said Claire in a flirtatious way not for herself but for her stepsister, Athena.

"What?" asked DJ as though he was surprised and had just received good news.

"You mean dat the pretty girl with the long hair?" asked DJ.

"Yep," replied Claire.

DJ was thinking to himself: *'That girl is cute and fine. I wonder if she'll meet me somewhere.'*

"Tell her to meet me at Mrs. Goodman's house in an hour," said DJ.

"Okay," said Claire as she began to run back home very fast and without even saying goodbye.

Mrs. Goodman was the neighborhood house where all the kids gathered and just hung out. She had a beautiful lawn with loads of scenic flowers. Mrs. Goodman was outgoing and had a pleasant demeanor about herself. Mrs. Goodman would also sell candy, cookies, and pickles to the children for a little of nothing.

While back at the stepmom's house, Athena was tired from working and knew that when she'd finished the dishes, she had to sweep the floors and mop and dust furniture. She also had to help her other siblings with their homework and do her homework as well. Then, she had to get them ready for bed and their clothes ready for school the next morning.

Suddenly, Claire, the younger stepsister returned to the house and went directly into the kitchen where Athena was tirelessly working.

"Guess what?" asked Claire.

"Girl, I don't have time fa yo mess," said Athena.

"Oh, it ain't no mess," said Claire.

"Mh hmmmm," said Athena.

"Guess who I just talked to?" asked Claire.

"Who, girl?" asked Athena.

"DJ," said Claire.

Athena stopped abruptly of what she was doing and her entire face started to glow with joy.

"What did he say? What did he say?" asked Athena insistently.

"He wants you to meet him at Mrs. Goodman's house in an hour," said Claire.

Both Claire and Athena began to jump with joy and in circles, as the good news was a welcoming message.

"But I have to finish these dishes and mop and dust," said Athena.

"I'll finish until you git back. Mom is gone to sleep on da couch in da living room. Just be quiet," said Claire.

25

"Okay, I'm going to put on some of Ms. Jeans' lipstick and wash under my arms," said Athena as she returned to dishwashing, but at a much faster pace. Claire had gotten the broom and started to sweep to speed up the process.

After a while, Athena snuck passed her sleeping stepmother and into her bedroom to sneak on her lipstick. She even put lipstick on her cheeks to give her face a little color. She combed her long, luscious hair. She dashed to the bathroom and wet a towel with soap and water and began to wipe under her armpits. She snuck back into her stepmother's room and dashed on a little perfume. She was careful not to use too much in fear that her stepmom may notice. She went back into the kitchen where Claire was beginning to mop. Once there, she asked Claire for her opinion.

"How do I look?" asked Athena.

"Ouuuuu-weeee! You look cute," said Claire with excitement.

"Okay, don't wake Ms. Jean up and I'll be back soon," said Athena.

"Okay," said Claire.

One Hour Later

Athena was now approaching Mrs. Goodman's house. DJ wasn't there yet, so she began to admire the beautiful arrangements of flowers that were in the yard. She waited anxiously, as fifteen minutes had passed after the hour they were supposed to have met. She thought to herself that she really wanted to see DJ, but if her stepmother awoke and found her missing, she'd have to pay the consequence, which could mean a whipping with a switch and without clothes on by her stepmom.

Just as she had almost talked herself into leaving in fear of her stepmother awaking, DJ approached her from behind.

"Hey, girl," he said as he frightened her. He looked great and smelled good as though he had snuck on some of his dad's cologne. His hair was neatly combed and he was not wearing the clothes he'd had on when he was cutting the lawn earlier. His skin was so fair and light almost like white people because he had some French in his blood. His hair was straight like white people as well and he had an athletic build to top it off. Athena was smitten and tried not to show it.

"Hey, girl," said DJ as he tapped her on the shoulder.

"Oh, hey," said Athena as she was relieved to see him. They both began to laugh.

"You scared me," she said as he continued to laugh.

"What's your name?" he asked.

"Athena," she replied.

"What's your name?" she asked.

"Donald, but everyone calls me DJ," he replied.

"I never thought you even noticed me," said Athena.

"You don't have to see the sun to know it's shinning," replied DJ as Athena felt warm inside and smiled within. It was a feeling she'd never felt before. It was the attention she'd never received before either. It was the best compliment she'd ever received in her life. Someone, as good-looking as DJ, noticed her. Athena was smitten and DJ fell hard for Athena in return. Puppy love was what it was called back in the day. Infatuation is what we call it today.

Donald and Athena made a lot more small conversations and as it was beginning to get dark, Athena needed to leave because she didn't want to get into trouble. She advised DJ that she needed to leave. He advised her that he would walk her home.

Now, DJ knew where Athena lived. Once they were near the house, Athena advised him that he didn't have to walk her completely home. Athena told DJ that the certain location, about a block from the house, would be okay and that he could turn around and go back home. '*Just don't walk me to the front porch,*' she'd advised him. Athena was in fear of her stepmother seeing them together.

"You don't have to walk me no further, DJ," said Athena.

"Okay," said DJ.

"May I call you sometime?" asked DJ.

"Yeah, my number is 555-3234. Can you remember dat?" asked Athena. She'd given DJ the telephone number to her real mother's house in fear that her stepmom may talk ugly to him. Her stepmom hated light-skinned black people. Maybe it was because she was so dark-skinned.

"Oh yeah, I'll remember it," DJ replied.

Athena abruptly broke away from DJ before he tried to kiss her and began running toward the front porch. They waved their goodbyes as Athena snuck back into the house. Her stepmother was still asleep on the couch.

Athena was relieved that her stepmother had never awakened and she ran back into the kitchen where Claire was continually cleaning.

"Did you see him? Did you see him?" Claire anxiously asked.

"Yes, yes, yes, he's so cute and he asked me for my phone number," replied Athena.

Both girls began to jump and scream but abruptly stopped in fear of awakening Mrs. Jean, Athena's stepmother. They began to laugh and play together with excitement.

"Did he kiss you? Did he kiss you?" asked Claire.

"No, he wanted to, but I ran in the house before he could," said Athena as both girls began to laugh and play again quietly.

Athena then ran into the bathroom and began taking off the lipstick and rubbed off the perfume. She didn't want any evidence that she had been out. She even disarrayed her hair as though she had been cleaning the entire time. She relieved Claire of her duties and continued to clean, thinking of DJ the entire time with a smile on her face.

Weeks Later

Now, Athena was at her real mother's house, Mrs. Harriet. For the next two weeks, DJ and Athena talked on the telephone. The telephone rang.

"Hello," said Mrs. Harriet Murray.

"Hello, ma'am, may I speak with Athena?" asked DJ.

"Hold on," said Mrs. Harriet Murray.

"Athena, telephone, gal," she said. Athena knew fully well of who was on the other end of the telephone and Athena didn't want to alert her mother of her happiness.

"Hello," said Athena as she answered the phone.

"Hey, baby," said DJ.

Athena was all semi-smiles as her mother was watching and listening. Her mother too notices Athena's glaring attitude. Athena whispers quietly and makes the conversation quick when her mother's around. Yet, her mom knows all too well what Athena's up to.

Athena and DJ

Athena and DJ, or Donald, continued their relationship as they learned about each other's family history. DJ told her that he had been adopted because his real mother had gotten pregnant when she was only twelve years old. His mother couldn't keep him and it would have been an embarrassment to the family, so she was sent off to a relative's house and gave birth. Another relative, who had been barren, adopted him and had given him a good life. He attended Our Lady of the Blessed Sacrament School and was very well educated. He lived in a nice home and had some of the finer things in life when most blacks couldn't afford such living.

Our Lady of the Blessed Sacrament Academy was a school for African-American Catholic children. It was run by several nuns and a diocese. The nuns were strict and did not spare the rod. They also had what was known as 'The sacrament of confirmation' which is 'baptism and Eucharist,' one of the three sacraments of initiation; *confirmation* completes the grace of baptism. Catholic children were the first to wear uniforms, as they stood out as being special. It also cost money for a child to attend Blessed Sacrament, which meant you had it to spare.

Athena, on the other hand, came from a broken home. Her father abandoned her when she was little and returned much later in her life after he'd gotten married to another woman, Mrs. Jean. It was years later when her mother, Mrs. Harriet, married Mr. Murray. Yet, before then, her mother and grandmother worked hard to feed her and Athena because welfare and food stamps were of none existence. Money was tight and clothes were few, but they made it through lots of struggling and just the acceptance of being without.

Resistance

They say opposites attract, but what seemed like an unlikely couple soon became an item. While at Athena's mother's house, there was some resistance by Mrs. Harriet about DJ. Mrs. Harriet also didn't like DJ because he was so well educated, had a good home, and loved adopted parents.

"I don't like dat boy you seeing," said Mrs. Harriet Murray.

"Who, DJ?" Athena asked.

"Yeah, who else is I'm talking 'bout?" asked Mrs. Harriet Murray.

"Why?" asked Athena in a polite way.

"He look like he white and he talk like he white," said Mrs. Harriet Murray in a '*put down*' type of voice.

"He's nice though," said Athena.

"Yeah, but I still don't like him. He thinks he cute and *he'll end up treating you bad*," said Mrs. Harriet Murray.

"He said he ain't never gone do dat," replied Athena.

"Mark my word, little girl. You need to leave him alone. He even acts like he white and I can't stand him," said Mrs. Harriet Murray.

Athena was very respectful toward her mother and said little to upset her. Deep down in her heart, she knew she was in love with DJ no matter what her mother or stepmother said or what they'd thought about him.

Athena and DJ continued to date, as they both were head over heels in love with each other. Athena tried not to let her mother or stepmother see them together in fear that they may embarrass her. Yet, the more she tried, the more both women knew very well what she was up to and with whom she was with. Mrs. Harriet Murray and her stepmom continued to nag at Athena about DJ as much as they could, to no avail.

Chapter 3
Athena's Marriage

Family

Wedding bells began to ring outside the tiny Baptist Church in Shreveport. There was a small group of attendees that had come to support Athena and DJ, Donald. Athena was twenty years of age and DJ was just shy of his twentieth birthday. They were madly in love with each other and felt in their hearts that it was the right thing to do. They'd dated since they were sixteen and felt it was the magical time for '*forever after.*'

Athena had made it up in her mind that she was going to be a better mother than Mrs. Harriet, her mother, and her stepmother, Mrs. Jean. She also had made it up in her mind that she was going to treat DJ with respect so that their children would always have a dad, a decent provider, unlike her family life. She envisioned having many children for this handsome man because he was so good-looking as they were living '*happily ever after.*' She just knew that her children would be beautiful because he was so light-skinned and handsome.

If children were what Athena wanted, children were what she got, nine in all. Athena and DJ ended up having five boys and four girls. Their third child was a girl and her name was Samantha. There was something special about Samantha. She had an inner beauty and strength that was different from all the other children. She seemed tough as nails and rarely got sick.

Trouble in Paradise

Tensions had become apparent in Athena and DJ's marriage. There was hardly ever enough money to make ends meet, ever. To add to the problems the couple already had, Athena and DJ began to drink heavily. They would fuss and fight to no end. They had to move constantly because of mismanagement of funds. Back then, 'welfare' was of non-existence as well as food stamps. So, whatever funds DJ made were all the funds the family had because Athena was a stay-at-home mom and understandably so, with nine small children.

Athena

Athena thought that the life she'd once known with her mean mother and stepmother was bad until she and DJ began to go through difficult times themselves. DJ had become mentally and physically abusive toward her. Athena had become depressed and DJ's treatment toward her eventually drove her to drinking. Athena had become a severe alcoholic. Because there wasn't enough money to make ends meet, there wouldn't be enough funds to pay the light and water bills. To add insult to injury, the couple would be evicted every month, literally.

Athena could only remember her mother telling her about DJ, '*He'll treat you bad.*' This vision kept ringing in her mind over and over again, which gave her an excuse to drink, so she thought. She'd had enough children, like her mother, to do her housework for her. Athena remembered telling herself she'd never be like her mother, only to not realize she'd become worse than her mother in so many other ways.

DJ

DJ was brought up privileged. He'd gone to private schools and always had a roof over his head and plenty of food to eat. DJ had never known struggling and being without growing up.

As a younger child, DJ envisioned having a wife and a couple of children that were being well taken care of and happy. He'd envisioned his children being chaperoned to catholic schools and dressed neatly in uniforms as he'd once lived. He'd looked forward to a beautiful life with Athena and could see the two of them living a '*happily-ever-after*' lifestyle.

DJ couldn't cope with the present situation that he was in with Athena and family now. Being gone on the highway with his job was like a refresher for him. He'd rather be away driving eighteen-wheelers than at home with his nagging wife and unprovided family. He'd wanted so much more for them but didn't have the funds to do so.

Not being home with family meant that his children would suffer the consequences. It meant that they would be home with drinking and depressed Athena. It seemed that both had other problems, and if you think the children didn't notice, they did.

DJ also was used to his lifestyle being in an orderly fashion. He had both parents that cared for him and after-school functions to help him excel in life. He also learned discipline, as he had chores to do around the house like cutting the lawn and taking out the trash. He wasn't accustoming to this type of living which only depressed him and ultimately made him an alcoholic.

Having nine mouths to feed only added to his melancholic state. He loved each and every one of his children, but being an only child, sharing was something out of his league. It seemed the more he'd work, the less money he had.

Chapter 4
Samantha

Samantha

Samantha was Athena and DJ's third child. She was born in 1965 and was healthy and beautiful. There was something special about Samantha. She was like a rose that was ready to bloom before its time. She had an unspoken strength about her that was simply unexplained.

Athena was a stay-at-home mom while DJ was the breadwinner. This meant that DJ was on the road for long periods of time, as he'd gotten a job driving eighteen-wheelers. Money was always tight, but manageable, at first.

Soon, there was a strain in the marriage and cracks were becoming apparent. Being on the road frequently, DJ had begun to indulge in alcohol, ceaselessly so. He would often come home drunk as the couple would argue and engage in pushing battles whenever he was home. Athena stayed pregnant, it seemed, and more strains were forthcoming.

Samantha as a Small Child

Like most four-year-olds, Samantha loved to sing, jump, run, and dance. She was smart and would take notice of all her surroundings. Questions were asked by Samantha, as it was in her nature to want to explore new surroundings.

One day, while DJ was at work, Samantha, at age four, walked into another room and stumbled upon her mother and DJ's friend, Mr. Felix as the children would call him, together. They were hugged up and about to kiss when Samantha walked in on them. Samantha felt and thought it was strange that her mother was hugged up with another man other than her dad. The funny look on Samantha's face indicated that even though she was only four,

Samantha knew it was wrong. Maybe it was perhaps the 'tree of knowledge of good and evil,'[2] referring to the story of Adam and Eve. Samantha now had been thrown into a world bled of color and meaning.

DJ, to Samantha, had accumulated numerous affairs himself but was never caught in them. Yet, DJ had always suspected Athena of having an affair with his friend; he just didn't have the proof though. This led to many arguments and sleepless nights for the family. This also led to more alcohol abuse between Athena and DJ. One particular day, in the early hours of the morning, Samantha remembered,

"Why you keep coming home late, DJ?" asked Athena.

"I was at work," said DJ.

"It don't take dat long on your job. I know yo schedule. You wit somebody else. I know it," Athena said accusingly.

"All you do is complain and complain. Why don't you git up off yo behind and do some work yourself instead of making these kids do all da work," asked DJ.

"You don't tell me what to do," said Athena.

"You my wife. I'll tell you what to do when I git ready," said DJ.

"Tell you girlfriend I got her number," said Athena.

"I ain't got no girlfriend," said DJ.

"So you say. I know better," said Athena.

"You oughta know better, 'cause I hear Felix's been hanging around my house all da time," said DJ.

"He ain't been here. Whoever told you, dey just lying," said Athena.

"Dey ain't lying. I know he's been here," said DJ.

"No, he ain't," said Athena.

"You lying," said DJ.

"How you know you be with your girlfriend and dat's why we ain't got enough money to pay these bills," said Athena.

"I ain't got no girlfriend," said DJ. If DJ had had a good English education in the past, he sure had lost his grammar over the years.

This went on all night long and the name-calling was not exempt. The children were afraid and tired. They were hungry and weary. The older ones would get up to stop the younger ones from crying, as they would continuously cry from the mere lack of rest.

Samantha at Age Four

One day, four–year-old Samantha and her five-year-old friend were in their beds resting or taking a nap. A very close grown male relative entered their room and her friend, who was one year older than Samantha, jumped up and ran out of the room quickly. Samantha wondered '*why*.' Now, no one else was present in the room except her and the close relative. The close relative had begun to touch and massage Samantha between her legs and in her private areas as she lay still and frozen. Her mind just wandered into nowhere. She couldn't scream '*stop*,' for she was dearly afraid, and he'd told her to be very quiet. She was confused because he wasn't hurting her, so she really couldn't scream. She only felt awkward. He'd told her that it was '*their*' little secret. Somehow, even at the age of four, Samantha knew it was wrong, for she'd felt it in her spirits.

Samantha realized that her close male relative must have been molesting her friend as well, but the two didn't reveal it to each other for a while to come. Her friend had soon developed a very low self-esteem and just accepted it. Whoever their close relative could catch alone was the one he'd molest at first, and then he'd escalated to rape. Being so young, they just didn't know how to discuss the matter amongst each other or anyone else, for a secret meant a secret to children.

This male relative started molesting Samantha at age four or as far as she could remember and then he graduated to him giving oral sex to her. Soon, she'd give oral sex to him. He'd graduated even further and started raping her in her anus. He'd use *Vicks Vapor rub* to get rid of the odor that comes along with sex. Samantha revealed that being so young, it would hurt so badly. Ultimately, he'd graduated to having vaginal sex and the vapor rub came along with it. Samantha and her friend, it seemed to Samantha, just took the abuse as though it was useless to defend themselves because of their ages. It was incest and rape, no doubt about it.

Soon, after many months of molestations and rapes, Samantha decided to confide in her mother about this close relative once the issue was pushed. It had become apparent to Athena that something was wrong with her daughter. Athena approached her and asked her a series of questions.

"Samantha, you haven't been eating lately. What's wrong?" Athena asked.

"Nothing," Samantha said.

"You sure?" Athena asked.

"Yea," replied Samantha.

"I noticed you been mighty quiet lately too. Are you sure you're okay?" asked Athena.

"Yeah, but this man keeps touching me down there and taking my clothes off," said Samantha as she pointed to her private parts.
"He told me not to tell nobody because it was a little secret," said Samantha. Athena knew exactly who Samantha was talking about.

"What? You better not tell your daddy 'cause he might leave us and not come back. You don't want that, do you?" asked Athena.

"No," replied Samantha sadly. It was sadder that her mother didn't get angry with this close relative for what he'd done to her innocent child. At first, Samantha thought her mother was going to say, *You better tell your dad, 'cause he will kill him for doing that to you,'* but on the contrary, it didn't happen as she'd presumed.

Samantha loved her dad and she never wanted him to leave and never come back, she'd felt. Little did she know that her dad would have indeed killed this close relative for doing such a thing to his beloved daughter. Samantha was too young to realize it and trusted that her mother was right in what she'd said. By her dad being always gone driving eighteen-wheelers, her mom was the one that was always home and Samantha feared that there would be consequences to pay if she'd told him about the sexual assaults.

From a Little Girl's Eyes

Samantha also was hoping that her mother would be upset enough to confront this close male relative about his wrongdoings. Samantha was confused as to what was right and what was wrong. If her mother allowed it, could it be okay even if it felt uncomfortable? Samantha wondered if all four-year-olds had to endure sexual assault and maybe it was just a part of life. She just wanted her mother to take her side and to tell him to stop, to hurt *him* badly as he'd hurt her, and most of all, for him to not ever touch her again.

The most appealing things about children are their innocence and openness to loving and being loved. It is also their playfulness and their innate humor that makes a child a child. It is simply their physical inward beauty. Samantha's innocence was deeper than Athena's ignorance.

Athena went on that day as though Samantha never said a word about the incest. The older Samantha became, the more she realized that her mother should have been her protector and stopped the molestations from her close relative at all costs. This didn't happen and Samantha resented her mother for years to come.

Chapter 5
Behaviors

Observations

Athena seemed to have ignored the warning signs that Samantha had been sexually abused by a close relative that had never lived with them and who was not Samantha's brother. There are signs that you and your family can take heed of and they must be noted to save your child from these predators. Many of the physical and behavioral signs of sexual assault are as follows:

Dianna

- *Behavioral signs:*
  Changes in hygiene, such as refusing to take a bath or constantly bathing excessively
  Develops obsessive phobias
  *Displays symptoms of melancholy, depression, or **post-traumatic stress disorder***
  Demonstrates suicidal opinions, especially in teenage years
  Has difficulties in school, such as nonattendances, or grades begin to drop
  Unsuitable sexual understandings or conduct
  Bad dreams or bedwetting
  Unduly overprotectiveness and worry for siblings, or impersonates a caretaker role
  Repeated regressive performance, such as thumb-sucking
  Repeatedly running away from residence or educational institution

- *Self-harms*
  Diminishes or appears terrorized by physical exposure
- *Physical signs:*
  Protuberance or swelling in genital area, bruises, bleeding, or bloodstained, ripped, or discolored undergarments
  Trouble sitting or walking
  Recurrent yeast or urinary infections
  Aching, itching, or blistering in genital area

The signs were truly there in Samantha's case, she admitted, and her mother must have known something was different about Samantha other than her not eating and being very quiet. She had shown signs of depression, post-traumatic stress disorder, changes in hygiene, trouble thinking in school, nightmares, and bedwetting. Neither Athena nor DJ picked up on the clues that poor little Samantha was silently screaming. They just didn't pay close enough attention or didn't care in Athena's case.

It seemed to Samantha that Athena allowed this relative to have his way with her. He was a fully grown man and should have been stopped. So, once Samantha had gotten older, she tried not to be available or in private with this male relative. The relative had molested and sexually assaulted her so much, and for so many years when she was young, that Samantha had become the wiser. Every now and then, the rapist would catch her alone and he would do his sneaky molestations and rapes with her as though he'd had a right to do so. Other times, Samantha made sure someone would be present so that he couldn't touch her.

The feeling of disgust and fear was upon Samantha when her incestuous relative touched her. She felt dirty, sinful, and empty. Her very childhood had been taken away as a little girl. Anyone who is a predator must, *must* get help and stop destroying the lives of little girls and women. If you have this problem, please, please get help. *'There is something wrong with you!'* How would you like it if you were small and someone did it to you or if someone had done the same thing to your precious little daughter? If you were a victim yourself, then you must break the cycle of hurt, filthiness, and slime.

Child sexual abuse can have future consequences and result in both short-term and long-term trauma, including psychopathology in years to come. Victims who have been abused sexually may rescind from school and social ventures and display various academic and behavioral misfortunes that encompass savagery to animals, attention deficit/hyperactivity disorder (ADHD), performance disorder, and oppositional defiant disorder (ODD). Adolescent pregnancy and high-risk sexual conduct may become visible in adolescence and child-sexual-abuse victims reveal almost four times as many prevalence of self-inflicted impairment.

Individuals that involve themselves with child molestation or child sexual abuse are responsible for a lot of mishaps in people's lives that goes on in the world today. It is my opinion and hypotheses and I can't prove it. However, there are many studies that have explained how an individual who was a victim of child molestation or sexual abuse, their lives have resulted in drug abuse, have led to crimes and could lead them to be a sexual predator themselves. Just think about the behavioral problems. We accept and just say, "Oh, the predator was molested or sexually abused when 'they' were a child." Only in these last few years have we, as a society, really made individuals accountable for their action before the statute of limitation expired.

Reporting

When a perpetrator deliberately injures a child physically, psychologically, sexually, or by measures of neglect, the crime is known as child abuse. Child sexual abuse is an embodiment of child abuse that encompasses sexual undertaking with a minor. A child cannot authorize to any semblance of sexual activity, period. Some operandi of child sexual abuse include:

Exhibitionism or revealing oneself to a youth

Caressing or stroking

Relationships or having intercourse with a youth

Masturbation in the company of a child or coercing the child to participate in the masturbating

Indecent phone calls, digital interaction, or text messaging

Manufacturing, owning, or allocating pornographic images or movies of minors

Intercourse of any kind with a child, comprising vaginal, anal, or oral sex trafficking

All sexual behaviors that are toxic to a child's psychological, emotional, or physical wellbeing

PTSD

Sexual abuse is specifically a menacing type of trauma because of the humiliation it ingrains in the victim. With childhood sexual abuse, victims are frequently too young to know how to communicate what is occurring and knowing how to seek out help. When not appropriately treated, this can have ramifications in a lifetime of PTSD, anxiety, and depression.

It is amazing that one out of three females and one out of five males have been victims of sexual abuse before the age of eighteen years. Sexual abuse impacts children and adults across ethnic, religious, educational, socioeconomic, and regional line. Usually, victims of sexual abuse will frequently venture to downplay their unexploited behaviors by saying that it 'wasn't that bad' and it's essential to discern that abuse comes in many shapes, colors, and sizes, and *all* abuse is detrimental.

Amazingly, when an individual has been involved in fierce sexual abuse (penetration, several perpetrators, lasting more than one year), detached symptoms become even more eminent. Research has shown that females with high subjection to child sexual abuse (CSA) suffer PTSD symptoms that are linked with deficient social undertaking, which is also reinforced by preceding research studies. The feeling of being 'cut-off' from peers and 'emotional desensitization' are both consequences of CSA and extremely prevent appropriate social functioning. Furthermore, PTSD is connected with a soaring risk of substance abuse as a repercussion of the 'self-medication hypothesis' as well as the 'high risk' and impressionable hypothesis. Lengthy, prolonged exposure therapy (PE) was found to plummet PTSD and depressive traits in female methadone using CSA survivors.

There are also physical consequences to child sexual abuse. Contingent on the age and size of the child, and the measure of impact used, child sexual abuse may cause internal abrasion, bleeding, and in acute occurrences, impairment to internal organs may transpire, which, in some instances, may cause demise. Child sexual abuse may cause sexually transmitted diseases and infections and due to the absence of adequate vaginal fluid, the possibility of infections can elevate contingent on the age and size of the child. Vaginitis has also been revealed.

Chapter 6
Incest

Child Incestuous Abuse

I, the author, am not trying to scare you but to scare you straight. This must stop and predators must be captured or called out for what's happening to little children.

Dianna

'The proper definition of child incestuous abuse is incest. It is between a child or adolescent and a related adult and has been recognized as the most universal embodiment of child sexual abuse with an enormous dimension to cause havoc to the young person. One researcher stated that more than seventy percent of abusers are immediate family members or someone very close to the family. Another researcher stated that about thirty percent of all perpetrators of sexual abuse are related to their victim, sixty percent of the perpetrators are family acquaintances, like a neighbor, babysitter, or friend, and ten percent of the perpetrators in child-sexual-abuse cases are strangers. A child-sexual-abuse crime or offense where the perpetrator is related to the child either by blood or marriage is a form of incest.'

Outcomes of Sexual Abuse

Without being said, the most conventional outcome of sexual abuse is post-traumatic stress disorder. Symptoms can expand far into adulthood and can incorporate unforthcoming conduct, re-enactment of the distressing event, evading of particulars that remind one of the incident, and physiological hyper-reactivity. Sadly, another spin-off of sexual abuse is that children abused at an early age often become hyper-sexualized or sexually reactive. This results in issues with promiscuity and poor self-esteem. These are regrettably recurrent responses to early sexual abuse.

Samantha had become a bitter child. She was angry at her mother, especially for not protecting her and her friend. She would always get into fights at and after school, and anyone who would look at her crossways, the fight was on. She'd always felt like a grownup because of the sexual assaults. Her entire childhood was filled with bitterness and hate. She acted out whenever the need had arisen.

Substance Abuse

If anyone had a reason to abuse drugs or alcohol, it would have been Samantha. I'm not making excuses for anyone, but an individual's childhood being taken away at age four because of sexual abuse just doesn't seem fair, but cruel. More specific symptoms of sexual abuse are:

Pressuring sexual acts on other children
Enormous of being touched
Disinclining to complying to physical examination
Retreating and distrustful of adults
A struggle communicating to others besides in sexual or seductive ways
Uncommon curiosity in or evading of all matters sexual or physical encounters
Confidential constituents to drawings and games
Neurotic responses (obsessions, compulsiveness, and phobias) Routine disorders (biting, rocking)
Suicidality
Unexpected sexual comprehension or behavior
Prostitution
Sleep difficulties, nightmares, and phobias of going to bed
Habitual accidents or self-injurious conducts
Declining to go to school, or to the physician, or residence
Secretiveness or unusual aggressiveness

There have been studies that have shown that children who have had experience of sexual abuse are inclined to recover quicker and with better results if they have a supportive, caring adult, ideally a parent, consistently in their life. This was not the case for Samantha. Samantha could have been an alcoholic or a drug addict, but she regained strength through Christ.

Dianna

'A pedophile's only true friend is the devil himself. The pedophile is the dirty one, not the victim. To take the innocence away from a young child is one of the most ultimate evils there is. It's a sick mind, a mental disease, and a crime. They should be locked up in an institution for a long time.

A good definition of a pedophile or pedophilia is a psychiatric disorder in which there is a grownup or older adolescent's involvement in a principal or unshared sexual attraction to prepubescent children. The fact that girls usually begin the undertaking of puberty at age ten or eleven, and boys at age eleven or twelve, standard for pedophilia extends the cut-off period for many prepubescents to age thirteen. An individual who is diagnosed with pedophilia must at least be five years older than the prepubescent child and be at least sixteen years old for the seductiveness to be diagnosed as pedophilia. For a grown man to molest or sexually assault a four-year-old child is disgusting and profoundly immoral.

Back in the 1960s, awareness wasn't an issue like it is today. Professionals are now more educated to spot out such problems in a child to see if they have been abused or sexually assaulted and other matters. Samantha was told by her mother not to tell her dad. However, she didn't advise her not to tell her teacher or a professional. Samantha was too embarrassed to tell her teacher or any professional for that matter, so she didn't.'

Chapter 7
Warning Signs

Stop It Now

Knowing if your child has been sexually abused isn't as easy to spot as you may think. One mustn't take anything for granted that your child is safe around close family members. Any knowledge or additional tips and forewarning signs of potential sexual abuse in a child's behavior will enable a parent to have a comprehension as to what to look for.

Dianna

'Any one symptom doesn't signify that a child was sexually abused, but the appearance of several indicates that you begin inquiring questions and think about seeking help. Keep in mind that some of these signs can emerge at other times of stress such as:

Alarming Indications of Potential Sexual Abuse in a Child's Behaviors:

- *Difficulties at school or with friends*
- *Other anxiety-inducing or devastating events*
- *In the course of a divorce*
- *The demise of a family member or pet*

Indications More Common of Younger Adolescents

- *Have other children to misbehave sexually or participate in sexual entertainments*
- *Imitates grownups, like sexual conducts with toys or stuffed animals*
- *An older child conducting themselves like a younger child (such as thumb-sucking or bedwetting)*
- *The child's new comments for innermost body parts*
- *Opposing to removing clothes at suitable times (such as bed, bath, toileting, and diapering)*

Conduct One May See in a Child or Adolescent

- *Unexpected mood shifts: fury, terror, insecurity, or withdrawal*
- *A child has nightmares or other sleep problems without a justification.*
- *Appears distracted or remote at odd times*
- *A child that leaves 'hints' that seem likely to instigate a conversation about sexual issues.*
- *Composes, draws, participates, or dreams of sexual or terrifying images*
- *A child has an unexpected change in eating patterns.*
- *Declines to eat*
- *Gains or radically increases appetite*
- *Has problems swallowing*
- *Instigates existing or uncommon fear of unquestionable individuals or places*
- *Declines to speak about a secret shared with a grownup or an older adolescent*
- *Believes self or body as disgusting, filthy, or atrocious*
- *Speaks about a recent or new older friend*
- *Unexpectedly has currency, toys, or other gifts without an explanation*

- *Displays grownup-like sexual behavior, conversation, and comprehension.*

Physical Danger Signs

Physical indications of sexual abuse are infrequent. If you witness these dangers, escort your child to a physician. Your physician can aid you into comprehending what may be occurring and examine them for sexually transmitted diseases. Danger signs can be in the form of:

- *A continuation or repeated pain during urination and bowel movements*
- *Discomfort, discoloration, bleeding, or discharges in genitals, mouth, or anus*
- *Wetting and soiling accidents independent to toilet-training*

Indications in More Common Adolescents

- *Anxiety, Depression*
- *Narcotic and alcohol abuse*
- *Sexual immorality*
- *Suicidal undertakings*
- *Terror of relationship attachments or closeness*
- *Obsessive eating or dieting*
- *Self-harm (burning, cutting)*
- *Insufficient personal hygiene*
- *Running away from the residence'*

Samantha, a survivor of childhood sexual abuse, explains the abuse due to firsthand knowledge. She wants to keep children safe from such predictors. Her vision is to have it recognized as a preventable public health problem.

It is Samantha's mission to 'stop it now!' It is also her mission to prevent the sexual abuse of children by 'mobilizing adults, families, and communities to take measures that protect and preserve children before they are abused.'

Yet, abusers can influence and manipulate victims to remain quiet about the sexual abuse using a number of different strategies. Oftentimes, an abuser will use their status of power over the victim to intimidate or coerce the child and they may even tell the child that the venture is traditional or that they enjoyed it. An abuser may make threatening remarks if the child declines to engage or proposes to inform another grownup. Child sexual abuse is not only a physical encroachment, but it is also an encroachment of trust and/or authority.

Here are some additional tips and signs of sexual abuse and some bear repeating:

- *Exceptional sexual conduct that seems unbecoming for the child's age*
- *Sexual acting-out on other children's private parts*
- *Genital itching, pain, bleeding, or swelling as well as sexually transmitted disorders*
- *Refusal to change for physical recreation, for example: physical education class or refusal to participate in physical recreational activities*
- *Melancholy*
- *Truant from home*
- *Terror of being in solitariness with grownups, especially of a specific gender*
- *Suicide endeavors*
- *Difficulty walking or sitting*

Chapter 8
Samantha's Hurt

Rebellion

Samantha explained that her close relative had taken some *'Vicks Vapor Rub,'* and every time he would sexually assault her, he would rub it between her legs. Samantha said it would burn so bad because she was just a child, but he didn't seem to care. He only cared about his selfish satisfaction.

Soon, Samantha started to rebel against her mother out of hate and lack of protection. When Samantha would get chastised for being disobedient, Athena would pull out a strap and whip and beat her. You'd think because Athena knew too well the feelings of unfair corporal punishment that she would never allow it with any of her children. That wasn't the case. As a matter of fact, she was worse than her mothers, Mrs. Harriet and her stepmother, Mrs. Jean. Samantha's heart was now unbreakable and had become hardened because of the molestation and of her hatred toward her mother. Samantha would never cry, as she'd gotten older, and when getting whippings, this angered her mother and made her whip her even harder. Yet, Samantha never cried. She just held her tears, hatred, and anger in.

They say that innocence is the growth of self-consciousness. Well, one day while at home alone, and when Samantha was about twelve years of age, it was her chore to wash the dishes. Her grown close relative surreptitiously entered into the kitchen where Samantha was.

One day, Samantha's abuse had come up behind and rubbed his private area against her behind while she was washing dishes. He was grinning and enjoying himself trying to get his arousal. At this particular time, Samantha had made it up in her mind that she wasn't going to let this grown man touch her in any way, for she'd had enough with his nastiness for she was 12 and old enough to speak out. Did he think that Samantha ever enjoyed his escapades? Of course, not, Samantha had never given him the impression that she enjoyed him touching her. He knew better and only looked out in behalf of his egocentric absorption.

Moreover, Samantha abruptly stopped washing the dishes. She counted from one to three to herself. Her blood pressure was boiling with hate. He stink to her and she'd hated the touch of his old, rough skin. His breath and teeth were nasty and old and his demeanor was corrupt and evil. She decided to grab a knife that was nearby. She turned around abruptly and took the knife and stabbed her close relative. He yelled like a little girl as he had the look of astonishment on his face.

The hurt this close relative had placed upon Samantha for many years, she'd tried to hurt him ten times over with one pierce. As a matter of fact, if she thought she could get away with more strikes, she would have stabbed him over and over again until the hate was no more. Yet, that one pierce frightened her, for she was a child and she thought she'd already killed him the way he'd screamed so.

"Girl, what did you do dat fa?" asked the relative as he faintly struggled to gain his equilibrium.

"I'm sick and tired of yo nasty hands touching me," said Samantha in a defiant voice. The relative slowly limped into the other room, being wounded but not mortally so far.

Samantha was afraid she'd killed her close relative. She was afraid she'd be on death row in a jailhouse as a murderer. Then, she thought at least there he would never touch her again and that would be all worthwhile. Samantha wished her close relative was dead, but not by her hands. At one point, she'd hated him so much that she didn't care if she indeed had killed him. On the other hand, she didn't want the stain of murder on her conscience for a no-good and sorry man like her close relative.

The fire department was called for the male relative by someone who'd seen him walking slowly, bloody, and struggling to get air. His bleeding wouldn't stop and it had covered him. The sirens were waling as the close relative had taken a seat at a nearby neighbor's house.

The relative was afraid that Samantha would tell the medical and fire and police personnel about the molestations and rapes of a minor. He feared he would go to jail and get beaten while there for the sexual assaults of a child. He walked about half a block from the residence where Samantha was. He wanted to be there close to Samantha so that he could antagonize and intimidate her into not telling their secret but was afraid she'd stab him again. He hoped so badly that Samantha wouldn't give up their little secret. Once the medical and fire personnel arrived, the close relative did what he'd known to do best – portray his dark depravity and evilness. He tried to assassinate her character in order to make her the suspect and him the victim.

The medical personnel arrived and of course, they summoned the police. Once the police arrived, they had to ask the relative serious questions about the attack. They questioned him, the grown close relative, as a victim of the stabbing and not as a suspect of sexual assault. Underage Samantha was now the young suspect with the assassinated character. The police really didn't get any answers as to what had caused the stabbing from the relative but only that Samantha was the rebellious perpetrator.

After all was said and done as people began to gather, no one else would call the close relative out as to what he really was, a child sexual predator, and that was the reason why Samantha had stabbed him in order to defend herself from molestations and rapes. Samantha's mother wouldn't even open her mouth and neither did anyone else who'd known the full story.

When it was all said and done, Samantha would be placed under the supervision of the juvenile division by a court judge. Because Samantha was so young, she had to be placed under psychiatric care. She also had to leave the residence and not return for a year. Samantha then lived with DJ's parents for a year. This was good for Samantha in so many ways. First, she could get three good meals a day. Second, she would get a good amount of rest. Third, she wouldn't have to see her mother or do major chores around the house, and fourth, there wouldn't be any more molestations and rapes from her relative.

The Television Host

Believe it or not, a familiar talk-show host that I will not call her by name has made a tremendous difference in the way sexual assault is reported today. She used her platform as a way to educate the public about such abuse. She was talked about, scrutinized, and tormented for doing such a thing. But that was okay for her; she really didn't care. She probably could have lost her job. Yet, she took the chance anyway because she knew that incest and sexual assault was wrong, and it must be stopped.

52

Now, it is mandatory for reporting sexual assault in a professional workplace, and police *must* investigate it because it's the law. If not, the professional can be arrested for not reporting it.

As it turned out, instead to her television show failing because of her stance, it prompts much success and we thank God for her. The media mogul outlined her own experiences with abuse in front of her television audience, which included being raped at the age of nine.

The talk-show host's risk-taking, unashamed attitude, and timely manner have helped millions of women and children avoid being sexually assaulted. There are cases that she'll never hear about when it comes to saving little girls. It was because of her unselfish, caring attitude and love that has brought women a long way. However, there is still much more work to be done.

The television-show host narrated being physically battered as a child, saying it was a cultural experience many African-American children went through. The host was raped and molested and she grew up in a surrounding where children were seen and not heard. At age six, the host left her grandmother to live with her mother, and while there, the female relative, being in charge of keeping the house, contrived her to sleep on the porch, and at nine, she was sexually assaulted.

Dianna

'The host was nine years old when she was first sexually abused. One day, while babysitting someone's children, her nineteen-year-old cousin raped her. Afterwards, he had taken her out for ice cream. He advised her to keep it a secret. She did as he'd said. However, this would not be the end of the scenario. As time had gone on, she would face more sexual abuse from a family friend as well. She kept silent about all of it for years.

So the host went to live with her father who was a strict disciplinarian. He prohibited her from dating, having sex, or any aberrant activity. What her father didn't know at the time was she was pregnant when she'd moved in. A couple of weeks after she had the child, the baby died. It was a distressing time, she explained, but both she and her father saw this as a great opportunity or a second chance to do things differently. It wasn't until she was in an acting workshop one summer that her sentiments about the situation appeared again.

The host said that she'd entombed all of her sensibilities about it.

She said that she really felt like that baby's life — that baby coming into the world — had given her a new life. That was how she processed it for herself.

Even after she'd eluded her troubled childhood, the host still faced endeavors. When she went to Chicago as a journalist, her managers said they had __no__ opportunities to compete against other dominant talk-show hosts. This didn't stop her. She continued to work hard and remain focused and would eventually take over in ratings, above and beyond the other dominant hosts.

After all of the sufferings and agony, she triumphed. She was thankful, she said, for everything that had occurred. She vehemently explained that she would take nothing from her journey.

The host further explained that everybody's searching for the same thing, that question of 'was I okay?' Everyone is looking for that confirmation, asking: do you hear me and is what I'm saying important to you?

The host says that she knows what it feels like to not be desired. She says that you can use it as a footstep to build upon great empathy for people.'

This host is more than a talk-show host, for she is an award-winning actress as well. She's a media mogul and a philanthropist, and many count her as being one of the most influential women internationally. Because she stepped out, she is now larger-than-life, successful, famous, and has great fortune. Even though life wasn't easy, because of her sexual assaults, God used her and her situations to reach out to those women and children who were going through it and to avoid sexual assaults from occurring to women and children all around the world, period. It was clear; her childhood shaped the woman she'd become and paved the way for women to be safe everywhere.

Dianna

'It's because of brave women such as Samantha and the host that many of us weren't sexually assaulted as a child or teen. It's even without realizing it how we've escaped the unforgiving loss of childhood from sexual assault. We were able to live a life free of despair and trouble.

Samantha revealed that she'd always wanted to be a virgin when she'd gotten married. Her selfish relative had stolen that rite from her. He was truly the thief of her innocence, the murderer of her dreams, and an administrant of her nightmares. She also revealed that a lot of women purposely gain a lot of weight in order to not look attractive to the opposite sex, thinking no one would want to rape or molest them. The latter is definitely low self-esteem and low self–image, and research has shown that:

The connections linking sexual abuse and the level of self-esteem, depressive indicators, and controversial internet use were examined and analyzed. Juvenescence who had been exposed to sexual abuse revealed reduced amount of self-esteem, more depressive indicators, and extraordinary amounts of controversial internet use in contrast with juveniles who had not been exposed to sexual abuse. In the path prototype, sexual abuse predicted lower self-esteem.

A child that has been a victim, including child sexual abuse (CSA), is an impactful element in the advancement of diverse psychiatric conditions or manifestations in both childhood and adulthood. Amidst adolescents, habitually reported sequelae involve sexual disaffection, licentiousness, and an immense amount of risk involving re-victimization. Hopelessness and suicidal conduct or visualization is more ordinary in sexually abused adolescents in contrast to conventional and psychiatric non-abused controls.'

The research study had taken a total of six hundred and ninety-five middle and high school students, four hundred and thirteen boys, and two hundred and eighty-two girls. They concluded:

'The ramifications of the existing study revealed that juveniles who were involved in sexual abuse are at a considerable risk of hopelessness and problematic internet practice. A clinical involvement of this study is that ministrations for juveniles who were involved in sexual abuse should embrace a mental health screening, mediations to uplift self-esteem, and internet addiction counteraction measures. Ensuing anticipated studies are required to further shed light on the formal relationships between youth sexual abuse, hopelessness, and problematic internet practice.'

True Story

One day, I, the author, Dianna Thomas, was working at the patrol desk as a police officer sergeant. It was the graveyard shift, 20:00 to 04:00 a.m. At approximately 02:00 a.m., a fellow officer came to me wanting to talk. I was all ears. He said that he and other officers had made a call at the residence of a young lady. We'll call her Denise just for this story. She had three children, two boys aged around nine and eleven and a little girl that was four years of age.

Denise found love with a friendly and charming young man. They had gotten engaged and the male thus moved in with her, since they were getting married later that year. On one particular weekend, it was Denise's mother's birthday. The family planned a two-day function that required overnight stay, for it was a girl's-night-out weekend.

Reluctant to leave her family, Denise's fiancé encouraged her to go and get away for a change to have a nice time with her mother and sisters. So, she traveled the sixty-mile distance and the family began their celebration. Denise had become very bored at one point and missed her family and fiancé and decided to come home early instead of spending the night.

When Denise had gotten home, everyone was asleep in the house and it was very dark and quiet. Denise took off her clothes to the point of nakedness. She wanted to surprise her finance and hop in the bed with him naked, for he loved those kinds of surprises.

Once Denise had gotten off all her clothing, she snuck into the dark bedroom. Her fiancé was awakened and said,

"Oh, my God! Oh, my God! Oh my God!" the fiancé said loudly and surprisingly. He seemed fearful and utterly astonished. Denise wondered 'why' to herself because her fiancé was already totally naked and in bed. There appeared to be no one else in bed because the covers were flat and didn't have a silhouette of another body beside him. She pulled back the covers from the bed and discovered that her fiancé was in bed with Denise's naked four–year-old daughter.

Denise was flabbergasted when she witnessed this tragedy. She screamed to no end for her fiancé to get out of the house before she killed him. He hurriedly grabbed a few clothing and ran out of the house.

Denise had gotten the police involved, firstly because he'd committed a crime, and secondly, because she'd also found out from her little girl that he'd been doing it for a while. Overwhelmed Denise just was so outdone and ashamed, for she'd trusted this young man to be her future husband. She pondered that he'd only wanted to marry her because she'd had a little daughter. Her little girl never told because of promised secrets.

When the officer was explaining this to me, he had tears in his eyes. He said the fiancé left before they'd gotten there. The officer said they transported the little girl and Denise to the hospital so that the little girl could be checked out. The tearful officer said that when he'd looked at the little girl sitting quietly in the waiting-room chair, waiting for the doctor to examine her, 'the little girl's feet didn't even touch the floor, she was so little.' The officer was heartbroken and so was I.

The fiancé had fled the scene but was captured by another agency. Customarily, the Shreveport officers should have extradited the suspect from that agency and booked him into the Shreveport City Jail. The Shreveport officers didn't want to go and get him to book him into our facilities because many officers had said if they had to go and get him, they would have killed him, literally. So, as a courtesy, the other agency had to book the fiancé into our jail facility.

The Psychiatrist for Samantha

One day, Samantha, at the age of fifteen, and her mother, Athena, had to attend their first session with a court-appointed psychiatrist. She had to because the juvenile courts demanded it rather than her spending time in jail for stabbing her male relative abuser. Her age played a factor in the court's rulings. Samantha was very nervous and anxious. The psychiatrist slowly questioned Samantha of the incident between her and her close relative.

"Samantha?" asked the psychiatrist.

"Yes, ma'am," Samantha answered.

"How are you today?" the psychiatrist asked.

"Good," said Samantha.

"How are you, Ms. Athena?" asked the psychiatrist.

"I'm good," Ms. Athena replied, and she never asked the psychiatrist how she was doing in return. The psychiatrist cleared her throat and realized waiting for a rebuttal wasn't going to happen.

"Samantha, are you happy?" asked the psychiatrist.

"Now I am," said Samantha.

"Now?" asked the psychiatrist.

"Yeah," replied Samantha as she was afraid to elaborate any further because her mother was there looking at her in a mean demeanor.

"Samantha, what happened between you and your relative?" asked the psychiatrist. Samantha looked over at her mother for some kind of expression as her mother was 'mean-mugging' her. Samantha felt very uneasy to answer the correct response. Samantha remembered what her mother told her and that was not to tell her dad about the sexual assaults by the so-called victim, the close relative, and her. Her mother really didn't go into detail about what to tell the psychiatrist, but her mother's expressions told the story. Athena had the look of *'you-better-not-tell'* on her face. Her mother had the kind of look on her face that showed there would be 'an instant whipping when she'd get home' on her face about what her relative had been doing to her for so many years.

"I don't know," Samantha responded.

"Why did you stab him?" asked the psychiatrist.

"I don't know," responded Samantha.

The psychiatrist was very smart and had figured out the reason as to why Samantha's response was what it was. She really couldn't ask the mother to leave because Samantha was a minor.

So, other sessions went on in the same manner, with unspoken fearful words. Athena made sure Samantha never attended the psychiatric sessions alone. Samantha really wanted to tell the psychiatrist, but she feared her mother's retribution. Samantha feared her mother would take vengeance out on her for the criminal acts her relative had done to her. Unfortunately, Samantha was only treated by the psychiatrists for stabbing her relative and not the sexual assaults.

More Trials and Tribulations

As time passed, Samantha was back home with her family. Samantha had good reasons for not wanting to return home. Samantha painfully recollected that at least every other month the family would be evicted from their home. Ms. Athena was always pregnant and mean-spirited as Samantha remembered many a times when the family didn't have food to eat or water to drink or bathe.

Once, the family had found the abandoned house that her grandmother used to live in years ago. The family moved into the dilapidated house. By age ten, Samantha revealed that she had learned how to hook up and steal the electricity and water from the city. By the age of thirteen, she'd mastered the skill. The utility companies are more sophisticated now, but back then it was pretty easy to do, she said.

Samantha could remember one night, while living in the grandmother's old dilapidated and abandoned house, looking up through the roof and seeing the stars because there was a large hole in the roof and ceiling. The roof was about to cave in and you could see the insulation and broken wood pieces aloft. The house was filled with mildew and mold, and the nine children stayed sick all the time. To make matters worse, Athena and DJ would be up at two to three a.m., fussing and fighting amongst each other, as they both had been drinking heavily. Oh, by the way, alcohol was cheap back then as well.

One day, Samantha had come home from school and had gone into the closet to put her few belongings there. A large snake that had been living there as well jumped toward her. Samantha screamed and ran to her siblings for comfort. Athena demanded of DJ that the family must move, and so they did, into another dilapidated house.

It seemed that at least once a month, Samantha would come home from school and when getting close to their residence, all of their belongings were thrown out on the side of the curb as the city marshals had evicted the family. As a matter of fact, the city marshals knew this family by name, DJ and Athena, on a first-name basis. It had become so embarrassing for the children and for that reason, whenever they *did* attend school, they demanded that none of their friends walk them home from school because they never knew what to expect and would be embarrassed of how the house looked from the outside.

Many times, conditions were so bad at one abandoned house that the family had to move into another abandoned house. One time, they found an abandoned hotel that had been condemned for years. This hotel was in disrepair and decrepitude. It had been deserted for years and most of the rooms had broken windows. They found a room where the windows were intact, not broken. So, they moved into that room. It was filthy, to say the least, but where else could they go? The entire family of eleven was now living in a one-room dilapidated hotel room. The hotel had mildew and mold and was continually dampened by the elements. There was neither food to eat nor water to drink, and again, Athena and DJ would fuss and fight all night, keeping the children awake. After all, they were all in one room together.

Wherever the couple lived, Athena would always try to send the children to school just to get rid of them, not to educate them. Sometimes, Athena and DJ would get into trouble with the school system because the children would miss too many school days. They tried to avoid this as much as possible because they didn't want child protection authorities or the police getting involved. Things probably would have been better if they had, but it would have been too much of an embarrassment for Athena and DJ to allow this to happen. So, they kept the family together, even though they couldn't afford them.

School was a sanctuary for Samantha and the rest of the children, whether sick or not. Many times, their living conditions consisted of improper sanitation, unhygienic environmental conditions, social, economic, health, educational, and cultural problems, and many hazardous issues. Where there are poor sanitary conditions and poor quality of water, it leads to illnesses like diarrhea and other waterborne diseases, affecting life expectancy of many black urban dwellers.

At school, Samantha could eat free lunch and drink unlimited water from the water fountains. The school environment was cleaner and had healthier conditions, much healthier than they had at home. Samantha loved school, but the children never stayed at any given school for any length of time because of the evictions.

There were several occasions that the entire family had to go and live at the Rescue Mission again and again. At least there, they were fed and housed with warmth or coolness. Yet, there wasn't any privacy for Athena and DJ, and for that reason, they would leave. The children loved the Rescue Mission, but DJ, being a man of stature, had to remove his family from this environment. It was like unlimited beds in open space, so open that Athena and DJ couldn't fuss, fight, and drink like they'd wanted to. When the lights went out, they were out for everyone. Sleep was what the children got for a change.

Every now and then, the family would receive 'needy baskets' which consists of canned goods, flour, bread, and canned meats. There would also be goodies for the children and they loved it, except Samantha. This embarrassed Samantha to no end to accept hand-me-downs all the time. She just longed for a stable family life.

Several times, the family would also have to live in DJ's eighteen-wheeler. Imagine a family of eleven living in the back of an eighteen-wheeler trailer. They had to use public restrooms at gas stations and had to wash up there as well. It was humiliating to Samantha. Her heart ached for a decent family life. In the summer, the back of the truck would me smoldering hot. In the winter, it would be freezing cold. One could hardly breathe at times because of its enclosures.

When the family did find a house to rent or live in, it seemed that Samantha would be the one her mother would work to death more so than her other siblings, she'd felt. You'd think that Athena, of all people, knew better because of the how her mother singled her out from her siblings to do all the work, not so. Samantha was the chosen one to do all the work which added more resentment toward her mother. Samantha was so unhappy in the life she had that she wished the Lord would end it for her. Yet, she'd had no other choice but to keep on living.

What a hard life a family must endure! It was a life not of the children's own choosing but one due circumstance. Samantha endured hardship after hardship and wished her life would end at her young age. She would often see how good other families were and she prayed that her family could take model after them. It never did, and as a matter of fact, it only got worse.

Samantha's Resentment

One day, while all the children were sitting around the house on a cold and rainy day, the subject came up about infidelity.

"Mom, what happens when a woman cheats on their husband?" asked one small child as Samantha intently looked on.

"Oh, dat's bad. I ain't never been wit another man," said Athena. Samantha looked shocked in as much as she knew her mother was lying because she'd seen her for herself with Mr. Felix.

Samantha also remembered her relative molesting her and when she'd confided in her mother, she rejected protecting her. This stirred up bad feelings in Samantha's heart because her mother had portrayed to everyone as though she was the faithful and dutiful wife and mother. Yet, in reality, she was neglectful toward Samantha, as she allowed a close relative to have his way with her.

Samantha also blamed her mother for not making conditions better for the family. She felt that her dad and mom only cared about drinking alcohol instead of a stable family life. She didn't blame her dad so much because at least he worked every day. It was because she saw her mom more often than her dad and therefore, it was her mother who she resented the most.

Chapter 9
Samantha Grows Up Early

Athena Finds Birth-Control Pills

Athena frequently called on Samantha, now fifteen years old, to do major chores around the house rather than her other siblings because she knew that if she'd called on Samantha to do something, it would be done at once. One day, Athena was looking through her daughters' dresser drawers and found a pack of birth-control pills. Without hesitation, she *only* suspected Samantha.

"Samantha," cried Athena.

"Yes," Samantha responded.

"Where did you git these birth-control pills from?" asked Athena.

"Those ain't mine," responded Samantha.

"Quit lying to me, girl. Where did you git 'em from?" asked Athena.

"Those ain't mine, Mamma," Samantha vehemently replied.

"So, you think you're grown now," asked Athena.

"I told you those ain't mine. Maybe they're yours and Mr. Felix's," said Samantha in a resentful and rebellious way. Mr. Felix was her dad's friend, whom Athena supposedly had been having an affair with.

Athena slapped Samantha across the face very hard that Samantha fell to the ground. Athena began to beat Samantha all over her body out of anger.

"Git out of my house, gal," said Athena.

"Git out," Athena said over and over again.

Samantha grabbed a few items, not knowing what to clasp because she'd never been thrown out of the house before, so she didn't get the essentials. Her other siblings looked on as Samantha ran out of the front door. Samantha was crying and all whipped up as she began to walk down the street. Her other siblings looked out of the window in sorrow for Samantha because they knew she'd hated her mother and that her mother worked her to death with all the chores as they'd continued to look on. As it turned out, the birth-control pills belonged to one of Samantha's older siblings and not Samantha.

The Lonely Streets

Darkness descended on the streets when the moon disappeared behind the clouds. Lightning slashed the skies, followed by a rainstorm and crackling thunder. Being lonely and afraid, fifteen–year-old Samantha imagined all kinds of grisly monsters about to attack her at any given moment. While lurking the streets, Samantha's heart pounded as she thought to herself of how she'd always been trampled upon. She wondered in sorrow of how some girls her age had taken for granted the simple things she never had – a loving family and a nice home, not a fancy home but just a secured home with loving parents.

Samantha wondered if all girls had to endure sexual assault as she had or if she was the only one in the world that had to endure such shame and pain. She wondered if her life would end on the streets by a murder or a wild animal or something. She was cold, hungry, hurting, wet, and afraid. Samantha felt used up and that her life was useless. She had neither money for food nor clothes to change from day to day.

By daybreak, the sounds of thunder had vanished. The sun arose and calmness returned as birds jubilated in the sunshine. The contrast between the frightening darkness of the night and the joy of the daylight was remarkably sharp. Yet, Samantha was still lonely and afraid. After being up all night, she tried to make it to an older brother's house. His house was now finally in sight as she stepped upon the porch and knocked on the door.

"Who is it?" asked her brother.

"It's me, Samantha," she cried. Her brother opened the door.

"What you doing here, girl?" her brother asked with very little pity, it seemed. Be mindful, none of her brothers was Samantha's sexual assault predator.

"Mamma put me out," Samantha explained as she was tearful, cold, wet, and tired.

"You can't stay here," said her older brother.

"Why?" Samantha tearfully asked.

"Why?" She asked over and over again.

"'Cause I said so. Naw git away from here," her brother said before slamming the door in her face.

Samantha cried aloud and continued to walk on another long and lonely journey. She didn't know where to go or who to turn to. She prayed to God, not knowing how to pray or what to say.

"Lord, I know I've tried to be good the best I can. Please help me. Oh Lord, please help me," cried Samantha. She continued to walk for another hour or two, not knowing which direction was the safest. To make matters worse it had began to rain again and was very cold.

"Lord, please help me in what am I going through, Lord," prayed Samantha.

Suddenly, a lady by the name of Ms. Diane spotted Samantha walking slowly on the streets as though she was lost and tired. Ms. Diane had many children, but she had a son about Samantha's age and they attended the same school. Ms. Diane was aware of the struggles the family has had to face, so she was familiar with Samantha's history.

"Samantha," said Ms. Diane.

"Yes, ma'am," Samantha cried.

"Is that you? What are you doing out here in this cold and rain?" asked Ms. Diane.

"Oh, I'm just walking," replied Samantha, for she was too embarrassed to tell her she'd been put out of the house by her mother. As Samantha had gotten closer, Ms. Diane noticed the scars and bruises all over Samantha's body. They then embraced each other. Samantha held Ms. Diane especially tight. It was a much-needed hug for Samantha probably because her mother and stepmother never hugged or kissed her. Samantha held Ms. Diane moments longer than the normal hug, for it was a feeling she'd never known.

Ms. Diane knew the walk, talk, and look that Samantha had when she'd first laid eyes on her.

"You come on in here, baby. You can stay with us," said Ms. Diane. Samantha had the look on her face as if to say 'how did you know?'

"Yes, ma'am, thank you," said Samantha very slowly and hesitantly.

"What happened, Samantha?" Ms. Diane asked as they began to sit in comfortable chairs. Samantha now had on warm clothing and they began to drink a cup of hot chocolate together.

"My mamma put me out fa no reason," Samantha cried.

"Awe, don't feel bad. When I was your age, my mother put me out too, so I know how lonely and afraid you were," said Ms. Diane as she hugged Samantha and wiped the tears from her eyes.

Ms. Diane felt sorry for Samantha and took her in as her own child. Samantha was no trouble at all for Ms. Diane and she wondered why her mother would put her out of the house. Ms. Diane was smart enough to figure out that Samantha may have been rebellious because of the family conditions, not knowing of the sexual assaults.

Many Days Passed

Samantha would always rush to do all the chores at Ms. Diane's house. It was second nature to Samantha. Ms. Diane noticed and had to slow Samantha down.

"Samantha," said Ms. Diane.

"Yes, ma'am," replied Samantha.

"You don't have to clean up every day around here. Just relax and do your homework or rest. Either me or my other children will help out on the house-cleaning," said Ms. Diane. Samantha was shocked, to say the least. She'd never seen her mother do housework, let alone some of her other siblings for that matter. Samantha's other siblings did do some housework but not as much as Samantha, she'd felt. Sharing responsibilities seemed to be not part of the family's repertoire.

This type of family life with Mrs. Diane allowed Samantha to excel in school. She'd gotten her proper rest, she ate good meals, and she had a clean environment to live in. Samantha would hug Ms. Diane to no end just to feel good inside. Samantha was slowly picking out the thorns from her body finally. She didn't feel trampled upon for once in her life.

Concerns of a Father

One day, at the age of sixteen, DJ came over to Ms. Diane's house to check on his beloved daughter, Samantha. He found her well-nourished, clean, and joyful. He questioned her about her leaving home.

"Sam, why did you leave home, baby?" asked her dad.

"Well, me and mamma got into it, Daddy," said Samantha as she still feared her mother's retribution about the sexual assaults and affairs.

"Baby, how are you doing? It's so good to see you," said DJ.

"Daddy, I'm doing fine. I miss you so much," replied Samantha.

"Samantha, I know I haven't been there for you all the time. I'm sorry for that, but I had to work, baby," said DJ.

"I know, Daddy. It's okay," said Samantha. She wanted to so very badly explain to her dad about her close relative sexually assaulting her ever since she was a little girl, but she was still afraid of her mean mother and the consequences. Samantha felt if she'd told her dad, her mother may make her come back home to live with the turmoil again. Samantha just couldn't risk it.

"You're stronger than your mom, Samantha," said DJ as Samantha listened.

"You know, here with Ms. Diane is a good place for you to be raised cause your mom was no good for you," explained DJ.

"I know, Daddy. I love you," said Samantha as they made small talk.

The father and daughter chitchatted for a moment longer and they said their goodbyes. DJ really didn't hug her because he, being an only child, really didn't have the affection he should have had within. Samantha watched her dad leave as he headed out of the door. She tearfully watched him disappear through the window as he had gotten into his car. She thought to herself:

Samantha

'If only I could have told him about my close relative when the molestations and rapes first began, maybe I wouldn't be the person that I am. I'm not caring, trusting, and I hate my mother for not doing anything about it. My mother didn't care anything for me. She never hugged me and never kissed me and she never even told me she loved me. Other mothers care for their girls and would fight to protect them. Not mine, not mine. I'll never go back home, never.'

Samantha lived with Ms. Diane and their family for months. Russell, one of Ms. Diane's sons, had finally finished high school together with Samantha. It seemed that Ms. Diane's son had a crush on Samantha. Samantha was too hardened to fall in love, but she was nice to Russell only because of the kindness of his mother. They'd become an item at school and around the neighborhood. Samantha felt she would never trust a man because of what her close relative had done to her in the past. Yet, she and Russell soon got engaged and then married. Ms. Diane was so happy that her son had found someone to love, but she really didn't realize that Samantha really didn't love her son to the point of being bubbly; Samantha only married him out of obligation to Ms. Diane.

Chapter 10
First Marriage

Russell

Russell was one of Ms. Diane's children. He was young, talented, and in love with Samantha. Russell was loved by his family and they supported him in all his endeavors. Samantha, not knowing the meaning of true love, felt that he really loved her in her spirits. He wouldn't have been her first choice if she had one, but again, out of obligation she'd dated and married him. The couple dated a couple of years during high school and decided to get married when finished.

By age eighteen and after finishing high school, the couple had gotten married. It wasn't a church wedding or anything like that. They got married in the living room of a shotgun, tiny house that they had previously paid for. Samantha's mother came. However, her dad DJ had refused to attend and felt Samantha could have done much better when picking a mate. DJ had had such high hopes for Samantha because she was the strongest out of all of his children. Yet, they married as other relatives attended the ceremony and it turned out very nice.

It was a perplexing thing; sometimes Samantha inwardly loved her mother but sometimes hated her just as much. She resented her for lack of protection. She aggrieved her for slapping her in the face and all the difficult chores she'd given her. She'd felt bitter toward her mother for making a difference between her and her brothers and sisters. All Samantha could think of was her mother telling her over and over again that she '*better not tell her dad of the molestations and sexual assaults by her close relative.*'

Ms. Athena would always bring up to Samantha about Ms. Athena being a virgin when she'd gotten married and how good she was by never cheating on DJ. Samantha knew better and saw it for herself as her mother continually lied to everyone. The only thing Samantha could do was to suck it up and keep it all inside. Her mother never knew Samantha's true feelings about how she'd felt about her.

Samantha revealed that she'd hinted to many adults in her family as to what her close relative was doing to her. She'd hinted to her grandmothers and aunts, and neither did a thing to stop him. This was in the seventies, of course, and things were a lot different than now. Still, something could have been done in hindsight.

Tragedy in Samantha's Family

One sunny morning, Samantha had gone on to do her daily duties at the little house that she and Russell shared. Suddenly, she stopped in her tracks as though a spirit had taken her back. She couldn't quite explain this unusual feeling, but she noticed it. It was stranger than anything she'd felt, even though it was only for approximately five to six seconds in duration.

The splendid life of Samantha and Russell was stricken with tragedy. One day while Samantha was at work, as she'd started working at the Shreveport Manor Nursing Home to make ends meet for her and Russell, she noticed her aunt and grandmother approaching the entrance. Samantha didn't think it was unusual because another female relative worked at the same place as well, but part-time. Samantha thought it was time for her other relative to get off work and that their aunt and grandmother were there to pick her up.

"It's time to go home, Samantha," her grandmother said.

"I don't get off until later, Grandma," Samantha said with a confused look on her face.

"You have an emergency at home," said the aunt.

"Emergency, what kind of an emergency?" asked Samantha.

"Your dad's dead," said the aunt.

"Dead, what?" asked Samantha as she and her other relative began to cry. Samantha began to run out the front door of the building and scream, as she was in shock. Her relatives and co-workers caught up with her and brought her back to her place of employment as they wiped away her tears. Later, Samantha was given a sedative to calm down.

Much to Samantha's surprise, her father, DJ, died in a vehicle accident. Samantha explained that she'd always thought he'd be shot or something to that effect. Never in her wildest dreams did she ever think he would be killed driving his beloved eighteen-wheeler.

DJ has had his issues with adultery, but he was a family man. He could have abandoned his family because of the dire situation, but didn't. Samantha had always remembered her father wearing shoes with holes in them. As a matter of fact, she'd never seen her father in new clothes at all. The holes were so big in his shoes that he'd placed cardboards in them to keep his feet from rubbing the ground.

The Family Hour

It was family hour at the Funeral Home Parlor. Instead of allowing Samantha's dad to be buried in his old worn-down shoes, Samantha went out and bought him a new pair so he could be buried nicely. While at the parlor, DJ looked peaceful as he lay in his coffin. He seemed so relieved from the turmoil of this life, Samantha said.

Russell and Samantha attended the funeral together, even though DJ and Athena really didn't want Samantha to marry him. They wanted Samantha to marry a guy named Monroe, who was a preacher's son. DJ never disrespected Russell, but he wasn't his choice for Samantha.

DJ had changed his religion from Catholic to Baptist. On a few occasions, DJ and Athena would try to take the children to church every once in a while. They'd joined a little church in the neighborhood once they'd stopped being evicted enough. This was the church Monroe belonged to and DJ really wanted Samantha to marry him. He felt that Monroe, being a Pastor's son, had good grounding and that Russell was raised primarily by his mother and stepdad.

The Funeral

Family members gathered at the church to pay their last respect to DJ. Everyone was traumatized at the tragic loss of DJ. They showed their feelings in their emotions and you could hear the screams and moaning that echoed in that tiny church, everyone except Athena that is. No, Athena was cool as a cucumber. It is a fact that everyone grieved differently, but Samantha thought that Athena should have shown at least a tear or two to no avail. Athena just sat and looked around the church very nonchalantly.

Later that day, after the funeral, Samantha approached her mother.

"Mom, are you alright?" asked Samantha.

"I'm fine," said Athena.

"Why aren't you crying about Daddy?" asked Samantha.

"Anything I had for your dad, he beat it out of me a long time ago," said Athena.

Samantha revealed that her dad, DJ, was the disciplinarian of the family when he was home and Athena was the good-timer. Athena disciplined only when she had gotten very angry and then it would be harsh. DJ was always at work and really couldn't be the disciplinarian as he'd wanted to be. Samantha found out that Athena's mother was so mean to her when she was growing up and that was why she felt she needed to have a good time *now*. Athena always had to cook and clean when she was growing up and now, and while raising her family, she was making up for lost time, even while being married to DJ. Her drinking and adulterous life was the end result.

Samantha's Grandfather

Once, Samantha confided in her grandfather, DJ's dad, a few days after DJ's death. She told her grandfather about the rapes and molestations by this grown close relative. Her grandfather said, *"Oh, I always thought it was DJ all this time that had been molesting you girls. I didn't know it was your other relative all this time."* Samantha was distraught over what he'd said.

Samantha

"You mean to tell me it was alright for my grandfather to allow DJ to molest his daughters and he did nothing to stop it? If DJ did molest us, which he NEVER did, why didn't my grandfather talk to him and try and stop him because it was simply the right thing to do? Why didn't my grandfather talk to us to find out if we were okay? Did my grandfather love his little granddaughters at all? I'd lost a lot of respect for my grandfather after that day."

Two Weeks after DJ's Funeral

Samantha was shocked to learn that *two weeks* after DJ's funeral, Mr. Felix, DJ's friend and the one person Athena had secretly been denying and having an affair with for many years, moved in with Athena. The children were astonished, but it was Athena's life and they wouldn't dare pick an argument with her. Many family members had lost a lot of respect for Athena after that, especially her children. Many of the children became distant to Athena and would not come to see her or support her later in life.

Chapter 11
Undying Love

Samantha's Pregnancy

Samantha was the first in her family, among her siblings, to get married. She started to attend church on a regular basis because it made her feel at peace being in the presence of God. She was introduced to Jesus in a personal way and she was taught the gospel more in depth. She learned how to pray and seek God, especially in difficult times.

The marriage between Samantha and Russell had gone on without problems at first. They enjoyed each other's company and Samantha was starting to fall more in love with Russell as each day passed. Yet, deep down, he was not her knight in shining armor, but she could live with the love she had for him. After the first year of marriage, things were beginning to change.

Samantha

"Russell became a very controlling husband after we'd gotten married. I couldn't wear any makeup on my face and he had to choose the type of clothing I had to wear. My father was the same way and it was like jumping out of the frying pan and into the skillet. Russell would neither let me wear a weave in my hair nor would he let me wear a wig on my head."

As time passed, Samantha began to feel nauseous and noticed that she had to use the restroom more often. She worked fulltime at a local job but felt very tired even after awakening in the mornings. Those symptoms went on for a couple of months and it was when she'd missed a period that she became alerted and made a doctor's appointment.

At the doctor's office, she'd learned that she was pregnant. Samantha couldn't wait to get home to tell the good news to Russell. She entered into the house where Russell was quietly watching the tiny television in the living room.

"Guess what, baby? Guess what?" Samantha asked with excitement.

"What, baby? What?" Russell responded.

"I'm pregnant," she said with exhilaration. Russell jumped up and ran to Samantha and gave her a big hug, as they were both excited that a child would soon be born.

Russell had always wanted a son to carry on his name. He couldn't wait for the baby to be born. The couple started to buy baby clothing, furniture, and little things that may come in handy for the baby. They started on a nursery of greens and yellows just in case they would either have a boy or girl.

One night, as the couple began to settle down in quietness, Samantha and Russell were in bed watching television. Samantha suddenly felt the baby quickening in her belly.

"Russell, Russell," said Samantha excitedly.

"Yes, baby," Russell responded.

"The baby is moving and kicking, Russell. The baby is moving," Samantha said excitedly. Russell moved closer to Samantha's belly as she placed his hand over her belly. Suddenly, Russell had a smile on his face.

"I can feel him. I can feel him," said Russell in an elated way.

"Wait a minute. What if it's a girl?" asked Samantha.

"Naw, he's a boy. I just know that my man is a powerful little boy," said Russell as they both began to laugh.

As week's passed, the galvanizing symptoms that Samantha was feeling early on from the baby had become worse. Whether it was a boy or girl, they were surely exuberant, Samantha thought. She thought this was normal because her mother would have these same types of symptoms – kicking and moving from the baby – when she was pregnant.

From being a little nauseous to increase in appetite, Samantha's body began to change. She had tender and swollen breasts, vomiting, fatigue, and lots of heartburn, but that was alright for Samantha because the bundle of joy would be worth it. Samantha felt that if her mother suffered through nine pregnancies, she could surely endure this one.

During these first few months of pregnancy, Samantha could feel the baby growing as her stomach had grown. She even began to gain a lot of weight, as she ate everything that wasn't nailed down. During this trimester, the baby grows faster than any other time of the pregnancy. The baby's heartbeat was apparent as she'd made her usual doctor's appointments. The baby's bones, muscles, and all the organs of the body were forming. At each doctor's visit, the baby was beginning to look like a tiny human being.

Samantha started taking prenatal vitamins early on and she'd added vitamin-D to help the baby to develop healthy bones, teeth, and muscles. She'd worked but was sedentary during most of the pregnancy and did a little exercise, not wanting to upset the pregnancy. Back then, this wasn't a practice, but now it's encouraged for women to stay active because if not, it may cause too much weight gain, gestational diabetes, pre-eclampsia, and varicose veins, and one was more likely to have shortness of breath and lower-back pain. Because Samantha had been sedentary, she'd accomplished the weight gain and back pain for sure.

In the first few months, Samantha felt the baby moving in her belly. The baby was getting heavier and heavier. The little bundle was even moving around as though he or she was trying to get situated. It was a beautiful time for Russell and Samantha as they basked into the goodness of becoming a family.

One sunny day, Samantha started to feel pain in her lower abdomen. It was a slow pain at first, but then it had become worse.

"Ag– Rob, Rob!" Cried Samantha as she was in pain.

"Baby, are you alright?" asked Russell.

"I'm hurting in my stomach. I need to git to the hospital," cried Samantha as she was in agonizing pain.

"Okay, baby, I'll get the car," said Russell. Samantha was placed in the vehicle by Russell very slowly. He drove her to the emergency room at the local hospital. While in the vehicle, Samantha prayed that everything would be alright, for she knew in her heart that it was too early to deliver.

After arriving at the hospital, Samantha was placed on the gurney by hospital staff and rushed into a room where there was a lot of surgical equipment. The nurses and doctors emphatically worked on Samantha to save the baby. She was twenty weeks along at this time. Russell called her relatives for moral support and prayers.

Ms. Athena showed up at the hospital. As some time passed, the doctors approached Ms. Athena to talk to her as though Samantha was a minor.

"I'm sorry, Mrs. Murray. We tried to save the baby," said the doctor as he began to explain emphatically. Athena wasn't emphatic at all because of the loss of the baby, though she seemed somewhat relieved, and this surprised the hospital staff as they watched on.

"That's okay, doctor. She don't need a baby anyway," said Ms. Athena. The doctor was taken back from Athena's response.

Russell overheard their whispering conversation and intervened between the doctor and Ms. Athena.

"What? What did you say?" asked Russell to Athena.

"I said she don't need a baby anyway and I meant it," responded Athena. As an argument began to ensue, the doctor intervened.

"Who are you, son?" the doctor asked Russell.

"I'm her husband, doctor. You don't need to talk to this lady," said Russell. The doctor was surprised because Russell looked so young and he didn't know that Russell and Samantha were married.

"I'm her mother," said Ms. Athena. The doctor didn't really know who to tell the confidential information to or who was telling the truth.

Russell stormed out of the hospital, as he had to go home and get the marriage certificate. Russell returned to the hospital with marriage certificate. Russell showed the doctor that he was indeed the major contact person for Samantha – her husband. The doctor asked Athena to leave, since she was beginning to start a lot of commotion. The doctor wanted the couple to grieve amongst themselves and in private. Ms. Athena abruptly walked away. She stormed out of the hospital and mumbled to herself along the way. Russell hated that he'd even called Athena in the first place.

Samantha was told the bad news by her doctor about the baby as Russell was by her side. The doctor explained that she'd lost her baby due to an incompetent cervix.

"What does that mean, doctor?" Samantha asked.

"An incompetent cervix or cervical insufficiency happens when a weak cervical tissue causes premature birth or the loss of a normal baby."

"Oh, okay," Samantha replied as she really didn't understand what the doctor was saying and only knew that she'd lost the baby. Russell also only understood that she'd lost the baby and knew none of the medical terminologies that doctors were explaining. Russell took it extremely hard and so did other relatives that were beginning to show up at the hospital. Samantha was sad but seemed to be okay with it and felt that the next pregnancy would be a success. She felt that if God had wanted her to have this child, He would have made it possible.

Samantha and Russell had to bury their baby in the nearby cemetery. 'Baby Mitchell' would be placed in a tomb at a small burial site. It was a time for Samantha and Russell to grieve. They'd realized that through this pain and sorrow, at least they had each other for comfort. Many tears were shed that day, but the thorns were just about to prick on a level they'd never experienced before.

Samantha's Reaction to the Loss

Recovering from the miscarriage, Samantha tried to give herself a chance to heal, both physically and emotionally. Each individual is different, but many women find that it can take a few days to a few weeks or years to recover from a miscarriage. For Samantha, the next few weeks would be a little difficult. Physically, her hormones were still raging in her blood, but her period returned as normal. The tiredness she'd once felt had begun to subside in the weeks that followed.

The ordeal really didn't bother Samantha too much after losing her baby, as she'd gone back to work to keep her mind abreast. Russell continued to work just to keep his mind on something other than the loss of his child, for he'd wanted a boy so badly. This painful and horrific experience seemed to have brought the couple closer together as they'd try again for another child after a short time.

Samantha's Second Pregnancy

Just as soon as Samantha's cycle retuned, four months later, Samantha was pregnant again. The couple felt that this baby would come to full term as they had high hopes. Samantha worked two jobs to help Russell pay the bills and to get much-needed things around the house. Samantha was determined to have a better life for her children than her parents and that was why she worked so hard.

At first, Samantha had taken it for granted that the first and second babies would be normal. After all, her fore-parents had had loads of children. Samantha said a little prayer to the Lord.

"Lord, please let this baby be normal and healthy," prayed Samantha. That's about the size of the prayer, something simple.

As weeks passed, Samantha again had gotten those symptoms of nausea, cramping, and fatigue. She started to take it easy again because she didn't want to lose this little bundle. She immediately took her prenatal vitamins as a precaution for the baby's healthy bones and muscles. The stomach cramps started out lightly and soon, they'd become severe.

The Baby Was Growing

The baby was growing and seemed healthy during the doctor's visits. Not really knowing much about an incompetent cervix, Samantha had begun to take it slow around the house and at work. She'd felt that there was nothing she could have done otherwise if her cervix was incompetent but to take it easy.

It was nighttime and Samantha and Russell were settled in and resting as they had begun to watch television.

"The baby's moving. The baby is moving," said Samantha in an excited way.

"What?" said Russell as he moved closer to Samantha's belly.

"Hey, little man, I know you can hear me in there. This is your dad. We love you, little man," said Russell to his precious baby. He felt Samantha's belly and placed his ear to her belly as though the baby would give him a sign of his or her existence. Samantha was so happy to see Russell happy again and hoped this one would be born a boy and healthy. She knew that it was what Russell had dreamed of for so long.

Twenty-Weeks Pregnant

At twenty weeks now, Samantha had begun to have severe stomach cramps. She had a sunken feeling in her soul and prayed:

"Lord, let my baby be okay," prayed Samantha.

Samantha's pains had now become severe, so she drove herself to the emergency room, with pain and all, to get checked out. She'd called Russell to inform him as he'd soon rushed to the hospital's emergency room to be by her side. Tubes and machines were hooked up to Samantha as the doctors and nurses tried to save the baby. Some staff members remembered Samantha from the last episode of miscarrying Baby Number One and they too hoped for the best for her.

The Thorn

The doctor entered the room where Samantha and Russell were anxiously waiting. The doctor had a somber look on his face and was hesitant to give them the results. Again, the doctors revealed to Samantha that she'd lost this baby as well because of an incompetent cervix. 'Baby Mitchell Two' would be buried at the same cemetery as 'Baby Mitchell One.' Russell was again hurt and this one hurt Samantha more than Baby Number One. Samantha was very quiet about it though and had taken it all inside.

The loss of two children seemed not to bother Samantha a lot until she had to attend a relative's baby's birthday party. There were lots of balloons, cakes, decorations, and gifts. Two and three-year-olds frequented the party and so did infants and small ones. Without an explanation, Samantha had to leave because the only thing she could think of were the two babies she'd recently lost. Things like this really bothered Samantha.

Moreover, Samantha indulged in the work of her two jobs. This kept her mind on anything but the deaths of the babies. She had taken care of Russell as well but somehow felt that his mind was somewhere else when they were together. She only chalked it up to the loss of their babies.

Samantha's Third Pregnancy

Several months later, Samantha was pregnant again. She was determined to have a child for Russell and trust that God would provide one. She slowed down at work as she had taken it easy, again. She slowed down at home with house chores as well in order to make this pregnancy work. Samantha had become desperate for a child after losing two babies already. Her prayers were now becoming more desperate as she'd prayed to the Lord again and again.

"My Lord and Heavenly Father, please, please, Lord, let this baby live," Samantha cried. "Let this baby be born healthy, my Lord, please."

Russell and Samantha were very relaxed and quiet in the bed on one particular night. Side by side, they were enjoying each other's company.

"Russell, the baby's moving. The baby's moving," said Samantha exhilaratingly.

"Oh yeah," replied Russell. Russell didn't even come near Samantha this time. Russell pretended to be getting sleepy, so he didn't do what he used to do – get near and feel the baby's movements. Samantha was very wise because of the fast upbringing she'd had. Deep down, she knew that Russell didn't want to come near her because he'd been hurt and let down on two previous occasions. Samantha was deeply hurt by this. She laid down and turned her back away from Russell and he had turned his back away from her. They were both hanging on the edge of the bed where they'd slept. Samantha began to shed silent tears and tried not to sniffle in fear that Russell may realize she'd been crying. He never found out how much he'd hurt her and she just kept it to herself.

While lying in bed, she couldn't help but think of how the thorns in life could come in waves and how she'd suffered so much in life while others seemed to have a carefree and rosy life. She'd wondered why some women could have children that they didn't even want while other women, once they'd had a child, would abuse and neglect the child. Most of all, she wondered why so many women would have so many abortions just to keep their lovely lifestyle afloat when she'd prayed to God just to give birth to *one* child.

The Prenatal Appointment

On the next prenatal appointment at the doctor's office, Samantha and Russell were somewhat excited because the saying goes, "The third's a charm." They'd placed their hopes that this third time must produce the birth of a child.

As Samantha was lying on the hospital bed to be examined, she and Russell were more afraid and less anxious about the birth of this baby than before. The doctor examined Samantha as he'd done an ultrasound and other medical examinations. The doctor left the room to check the results of the tests.

Russell and Samantha were quiet in the hospital room as though they were silently praying amongst themselves. You could literally hear a rat walk on cotton; it was so quiet. They prayed to the Lord separately and in their own ways. You could tell they were praying because each had their eyes closed and were silent as they waited for the doctor to return. "This far," the doctor explained, "the baby is fine." Samantha was about seventeen-weeks pregnant at the time. What a relief for the couple!

Another Thorn

Each doctor's visit became great hope until about the twentieth week when they'd become fearful because it was about the same time Samantha had lost her previous two babies. Week seventeen had now ended. Week eighteen and nineteen had passed also. It was so far, so good, as the saying goes.

To no avail, after twenty weeks of being pregnant, Samantha lost this baby as well. It was like one minute they were sitting around somewhat happy and somewhat excited in the waiting room, ready to see their baby on the ultrasound for the umpteenth time and the next minute there would be doom and gloom again.

The doctor and nurses hinted that Samantha should not try to get pregnant again, but Samantha knew that her God was the type of God who would give her the hopes and desires that were in her heart. He was the only God she trusted, the Almighty God, the maker of Heaven and Earth, the God of Abraham, Isaac, and Jacob.

Being shocked really didn't describe the feelings that Samantha and Russell felt. They'd thought of other siblings and relatives who could have children and lots of them. They were at a loss and chalked it up to the many rapes Samantha suffered as a child. Russell had begun to accuse Samantha of not telling anyone about the rapes and this would start an argument because she'd assured him she did. He'd blamed her and put her down, as he'd felt, for allowing her close relative to rape her.

Yet, it would be another sad day and time for Russell and Samantha. Yes, they had to bury this one too. Burying babies dampened Russell and Samantha's spirits. Russell had begun to lose faith and not attend church services as he used to. Samantha attended in spite of her circumstances and felt this was a time to cling to Jesus, not turn her back on him. She'd learned that whether times were good or bad, to love Jesus unconditionally.

The grave site 'Baby Mitchell Three' would be buried at the same cemetery as it's other siblings. Back in the day, Samantha explained that all babies were known as 'Baby Mitchell.' Now it's whatever name the parents give them. Three little tiny graves were buried close by and Samantha wondered what they could have become if they were born. She could only envision her babies playing in heaven together and this would bring a temporary smile on her face.

Dianna

'Naming babies 'Baby Mitchell' was probably a good thing for Samantha. If she'd named the babies she'd lost, every time she'd come across someone with the same name would probably be devastating to her. Yet, knowing Samantha, she would find her strength in Jesus Christ because she's that kind of person.

Samantha has revealed to me that other than seeing a psychiatrist for stabbing her close relative when she was twelve, she's never sought counseling, never. Samantha says that she only talked with Jesus Christ, and he's the one who'd bring her through the piercingly thorns. Jesus Christ yesterday, today, and forever was what she said.'

Many times, Samantha reminisced about the joy she and Russell would have brought their children if they'd been born. Samantha had known in her mind of how she would have been a much better mother than her mother, Mrs. Athena. She so desperately wanted to prove to God that if He would just give her the chance to become a mother, she promised Him in her mind and heart that she wouldn't make the same mistakes that Athena made.

Depression

Samantha was becoming bewildered and weary from the loss of her three children. She was tired and had become depressed. All of a sudden, Samantha remembered her mother being depressed back in the day when Samantha was a child. She remembered how her mother turned to alcohol to suppress the depression. Samantha saw it all too clear as to why her mother had turned to such vice. Her mother did it not because of losing children, because she'd had nine, but because of the struggles of life itself. Some thorns stick piercingly while others may stick slightly. That's how life is.

While sitting around the house and after losing three children, Samantha was tempted to go to the liquor store and buy some strong alcohol such as vodka. She remembered her mother in the vision, a vision of drunkenness and mistreatments her mother gave her. She now realized that since the alcohol had temporarily eased the pain for her mother, adultery was another choice she'd made to ease the pain of unfairness or hopelessness her mother suffered. Once her mother's affair sizzled out, more and more alcohol would come into play. Samantha's mother was a hardcore alcoholic.

With a hardcore alcoholic mother meant nurturing for the children would be out of the question. Since the family seldom attended church, Samantha didn't know who to turn to in this time of hurt and pain back then. The only thing she'd known was alcoholism and hardships when she was a little girl.

Samantha's depression could have very well led her down a terrible road. Samantha didn't want to travel on this road of no return. She was afraid that it may be a road that would ultimately end up being out of control and that she may not be able find her way back to a life of normalcy. Samantha trusted that God would ease all her pain, depressions, and anxieties.

Feelings of Failure and Guilt

Feelings of guilt and failure had permeated Samantha's soul. What she didn't realize was that it was very normal to feel this way considering what she'd been through. The mere feeling that a baby was in her care, inside her body as a fetus, forming into an infant and then it's ending, or death can be a very difficult matter to face. Samantha felt a terrible guilt that she was responsible in some way for her babies not being born. She questioned all the things she'd gone through over the last few years and wondered whether if there was some action that could have prevented the baby's brief term to end.

The Grocery Store

One day, while Samantha was shopping at the grocery store, she happened upon a woman who'd seemed to be tired and stressed. The lady has a shopping buggy and around the buggy were about eight children. Samantha assumed the children belonged to this unknown lady because they all looked like her. Samantha tried to be strong because she knew that she had to go to the grocery store often and there was no way to avoid it. Samantha asked God to help her through this situation because she knew that in every grocery store, there were going to be families and children and she had face this fact head-on.

There was no way around public places for Samantha, but God did indeed give her the strength to keep going on. After a while, Samantha had gotten over her fears of families and children and tried to live a good life, even though the thorns would appear every now and then to haunt her. It wasn't easy, but as time had gone on, it had become much more bearable.

Samantha

'I wondered if there was something that I could have done the last time or the next to tip the odds in my baby's favor. I questioned God but remembered an old saying that you should never question God, for He is the maker of heaven and earth and no one has the right to question His will. It didn't stop me from wondering though.'

Emptiness

Only those who have been through it really know the true feelings of the emptiness that Samantha was feeling. Sometimes, she'd felt complete and content while other times she'd felt less than a woman. To have the feelings of being a mother one moment and the next moment it all was taken away can be very traumatic. There would be times Samantha had a feeling of desolation and a gaping inner hole inside her. Her insides ached under the gnawing pressure of what seemed to be a profound vacuum.

A complete absence of joy, hope, or satisfaction had at some point and time overwhelmed Samantha. She now had begun to understand why individuals may turn to an addictive behavior. These individuals probably want to escape the emptiness and sadness they feel because of some deep and piercing thorn they'd had in their lives.

Even though Samantha had Russell in her life, she kept having feelings of lack of meaning in her life. There was an absence of true happiness or fulfillment that seemed to have taken over her soul. The loss of her soul, she felt, was manifested as the eternal sense that something was missing from her life.

Samantha

'*When the doctor announced, "Your test came back positive and you're pregnant," and as I'd thought I was a mother-to-be, it was such a good feeling. Then, to be let down by the losses and deaths seemed cruel to me. The planning and anticipation was euphoric. Being pregnant had it pluses as simple as individuals would open the door for me or give me a simple smile as they looked toward my belly. Then, the hope was gone, simply gone.*

The worst part for me was not knowing why this had to happen, the loss of my babies. I'd never done anyone wrong but always had wrong things done to me. I wondered if I'd forgiven my close relative as I should have, who'd raped me over and over again when I was a child. I wondered why God would allow a little innocent baby to die. I also wondered how I could carry a perfectly healthy child in the beginning and not to the end. Why? Why? How? How? When? When?'

Lots of questions Samantha had for God – why she'd suffered rape, abuse, neglect, and the deaths of three little babies. Do more questions like why 'surprise' us, make us 'excited,' and then shock us with loss? Did God receive all her babies and will their resurrected body be a fetus? Should she conceive again or not?

Questioning a God that knows everything is a mystery within itself. But those questions only led to anxieties, dead ends, and frustrations. Samantha had to cling to what she knew and what God has already revealed. Moses couldn't have said it better, "The secret things belong to God, but the things revealed belong to us and our children forever." *Deuteronomy 29:29.*[2] Therefore, we labor to entrust the 'secret things' to a mighty, sovereign, and awesome Father, believing He is more on our side than evil could ever be. One day, there will be only flourishing and happiness and not babies dying or children taken too young. Samantha had taken comfort in God's promises that He was with her, that He is for her and forever will be, and that He upholds her with His righteous and mighty right hand.

Grief

Grief is a normal response to the death of losing a loved one. For Samantha, it was both a powerful and painful experience. It was a series of physical, emotional, social, and spiritual responses to add to the list of feelings she'd felt. She really didn't have a good support team at the time and had to deal with it by herself in many ways. Russell tried to be patient and kind to her as he had allowed the process to unfold, but he had his thoughts and feelings he'd had to deal with himself.

Samantha had a different attitude toward grief than Russell when dealing with life's thorns. She'd prayed her way through the difficult times and it eased her pain. Russell was seldom home as Samantha would be home alone oftentimes than not. Their marriage was beginning to show signs of stress. Samantha confronted Russell to enquire of him having an affair. He assured her that he wasn't. She believed him and wanted so much to trust him. Just knowing the fact that she had a faithful and loving husband, Samantha could understand him spending time with friends and understood that it was his way of dealing with grief.

Samantha's Uneasiness

Trying to get pregnant again had become fearful for Samantha and Russell. At times, Samantha would find herself overcome with fear and anxiety that she may have complications in pregnancy or another miscarriage. Should she or shouldn't she get pregnant again was the question. Samantha wanted desperately to have a child and so did Russell.

There would be times when Samantha saw a loving family interacting; this made her feel hurt inside. She'd become envious, resentful, and unable to be happy for someone else when they'd announce their pregnancy or the birth of a newborn. It was especially difficult if the timing coincided with important dates in relation to her own losses.

Other times, an emotion would just hit her from nowhere or was unexpected. One day, while out eating with co-workers, Samantha was finally beginning to have a great time. When they'd finished eating and it was time to pay for her food, Samantha was at the cash register. Samantha turned around and *'bam!'* A pregnant lady was behind her. It ruined her day and no one ever noticed her feelings because she had become a master at hiding them. After all, she'd been hiding feelings since the age of four when she was molested and raped. Other times, she'd see relatives and friends who were pregnant and she resented them and they never even knew or picked up on her emotions.

The Fourth Pregnancy

Some time had passed and Samantha had become pregnant for the fourth time as her anxieties magnified. She didn't know what to think but was hopeful that this one would live. She had hoped that this one would lift the void in her and Russell's marriage that had become so strained. She wanted desperately for this child to live and she really wanted to prepare for its arrival as though it would, but was afraid to.

Samantha prayed even more desperately than before.

"Lord, I've lost three babies already," prayed Samantha. "I don't want to lose this one too, and I know what the doctors and nurses said. They said for me not to ever get pregnant again. But I trust you God, for you know the ways of my path and you have the final say. So... so please let me have a healthy baby, please!" Samantha prayed desperately as she cried aloud.

The Motorcycle Ride

One sunny day, Samantha and Russell decided to take a scenic stroll on his motorcycle to calm their nerves, especially Samantha's. As they drove out in the countryside, the scenes were magnificent. Samantha allowed the breeze to flow through her hair and skin. The weather was perfect and the temperature was nice. The air smelled fresh as though it were fresh linen.

Once, Samantha and Russell had gotten back in town, and after sitting on the motorcycle for a long period of time and enjoying the sunshine and fresh air, they decided to make a restroom stop. Samantha attempted to get off the motorcycle and she noticed a feeling of warmth that began to stream down her legs. It was blood or urine and it had soaked her pants.

Samantha looked down and noticed that the baby had begun to exit down her jogging pants as well. She panicked and screamed very loudly. She didn't have any warning signs that anything like this was going to happen. There were neither labor pains nor cramps that had alerted her of what had just happened. The baby began to move and she grabbed it before it hit the ground. Samantha felt its soft skin, as she was twenty-weeks pregnant and the baby had taken some form.

Samantha held and protected the baby as she and Russell headed to the emergency room at the nearby hospital. They'd felt that waiting for the medic unit would be too long, for they'd panicked and made a hasty decision. It was a short distance to the nearby hospital and Russell and Samantha felt they'd made the right decision.

While driving there, Samantha could only think within herself of her mother telling her after the loss of the first baby, *"She doesn't need a baby."* The thought kept ringing and ringing in Samantha's head and she was starting to believe it. She knew that God was able to do anything abundantly and above everything possible and this baby could be saved. She knew that if she'd put her trust in God, He would prevail. She just needed the faith as her grandmother had once told her.

Once the couple had gotten to the hospital's emergency room, they carefully rushed the baby to the hospital staff. The staff worked feverishly to save the baby and to save Samantha's life. The odds were against this baby being born, but miracles do happen. Samantha and Russell waited as Samantha was being checked out and cared for by the staff.

The Doctor's Report

The doctor entered the room with a somber look on his face and before he could speak any words, the couple had already known in their hearts they'd lost the baby. They witnessed that look from other doctors too many times to have felt otherwise. The doctor finally faintly spoke that she had lost the baby. This time, the doctor demanded that she not get pregnant again because it was now affecting her mentally as well as physically.

The doctors, this time, stitched her womb just in case that in the distant future she 'may' want to get pregnant or if it may have occurred accidentally. Maybe, just maybe, the next pregnancy would endure. Nurses advised her to never get pregnant again, and even though Samantha was determined, she was losing that spirit that she'd ever have a healthy child one day. Yet, deep down inside, she didn't care what the nurses and doctors had advised her. She knew that God was able because He said so in His Word.

The Evaluation

The fact that Samantha knew that her body had been lifeless, it didn't mean that God wasn't a good God. It only pointed to the reality that our world is fallen and in need of being saved. Samantha knew that being so close to death had placed her in a place to really see God's goodness more clearly in His provision of Jesus as He defeated death now and forever. With that being said, Samantha realized that everyone was already abundantly blessed through the gift of God's son, Jesus Christ. Samantha has firsthand experience of God's comfort, delighted in the truth of His Word, and rejoiced in His provision like never before in the past years. That was what brought her through her deepest dark days.

Samantha had taken the fourth baby's death to heart because she'd felt it and had seen it with her own eyes. That memory will be forever etched in her mind and whenever she'd see other families with children, she'd run alone to cry, especially tiny infants. Her heart was broken more times than any because families were many. This depressed her to no end.

Whenever there was a gathering at her family's house and Samantha would get into an argument with one of her siblings, they would always say hateful words to her. They knew just where to get her so it would hurt. They'd blurt out, "You no-baby-having heifer." They knew exactly where to hit her with their words that would count her misdeeds. Samantha would rather be hit in the head in a fight than to be called such mean names.

Strange Phone Calls

To add insult to injury, every now and then a child would call the house when Samantha would be alone at home.

"Hello," said Samantha.

"Hello," the child said.

"Is my daddy there?" asked the child.

"Who? Who is your daddy, baby?" asked Samantha. The child would then abruptly hang up.

When Russell finally returned home, Samantha questioned him about the incident, and he insisted that it was one of her relatives and no one he'd known. She wondered why the child would always call and either hang up or ask her certain questions. This went on for a while.

On another occasion, a lady called the house.

"Hello," said the unknown caller.

"Hello," said Samantha.

"B– that's why you can't have any babies. Me and Russell got a baby," the unknown caller told.

"I beg your pardon?" asked Samantha as the caller laughed and hung up the phone. Samantha was confused and hoped that her husband wasn't having an affair, but the signs were surely there.

Immune to Suffering

Envisioning a life free of troubles was what Samantha had dreamed of. The only other person she'd lost in her life, other than her babies, was her father years ago and she really thought that that would be the end to such suffering for a while. Never in a million years did she ever think she'd lose a child, let alone four. She questioned God as to how He could let her mean and cruel mother give birth to nine healthy children and she had to lose four. Samantha thought that if she'd had nine children, she surely wouldn't be an alcoholic, but instead how she'd bask in their love. It just didn't seem fair to Samantha to have so many thorns in her life even though she'd tried to reason with the matter.

Every time Samantha had lost a child, it only made her more grateful for the opportunity to be near Jesus by being acquainted with sorrow. She now had more respect for Him because He'd paid the ultimate price of death, Himself, on the cross. She knew she'd always be protected with loving ease and she found security in her circumstances with Jesus by her side.

Samantha's Fifth Pregnancy

This time, against the nurses and doctors' advice, Samantha was pregnant again. She'd prayed and prayed that this baby would be born. It had taken a toll on Samantha and her marriage. Russell didn't want to be near her at all, as if he'd lost interest in intimacy and the excitement of a pregnant wife having his baby. She'd placed her trust in God and continually attended church services to further find peace. She prayed for her marriage to get better and sometimes it seemed it did.

Samantha had gotten on her knees to pray to the Lord one day.

"Lord, please help me. Forgive me for all the wrongs I've done. Forgive me for not forgiving others who have sinned against me. I give my baby to you, my Lord. Please let this baby be born, please," cried Samantha.

Every now and then, Russell would attend church services, Samantha more often than Russell. Samantha knew that if she was obedient to God, He would soon bless her with a child. This would bring Russell back into the presence of the Almighty God and the family he'd longed for. She wavered sometime because she'd lost four children already and had to bury 'Baby Mitchell One to Four' at the same cemetery. Life was a funny thing to Samantha, for she only wanted two children in the first place and unlike nine as her mother had. She'd received more thorns than roses in life but just had to keep the faith.

Samantha wondered over and over again if her sexual assaults by her close relative had anything to do with the loss of her children. She wondered if her rebellion and hatred toward her mother had anything to do with it. She'd asked herself every question imaginable. She wondered if she'd worked too much to make ends meet and if that was the problem. She also questioned herself as to why Russell was never at home. Was it because there weren't any children running around the house? The laughter of a child or the energy that children can bring to a home, was that the reason her husband was never home?

To No Avail

Again, due to an incompetent cervix, Samantha lost this baby as well. She cried out to the Lord while waiting alone in the hospital.

"Lord, how long must I suffer and keep losing these babies?" cried Samantha. "What have I done to make you so angry at me, Lord? Give me strength to go on and not be jealous or envious of anyone with children, my Lord. Don't let me suffer, Lord. Don't let me get hurt."

Yet, Samantha did suffer and was heart-ached because of the loss of five children. It was especially true when she'd seen a commercial on television that involved children. It didn't matter if it was a hamburger commercial or a car commercial. If it had children, Samantha would be heartbroken. She would suddenly change the channel before the commercial would end or barely got started.

Vexation

Anger had begun to set in as Samantha tried to cope with the loss of her babies. She also felt frustrated and helpless as she'd tried her very best to take care of herself while being pregnant, to no avail. She had gone through the questioning of 'what ifs.' This matter was very heavy on her mind. She even tried to bargain with the Lord and promised to be a good Christian if He'd only let her have a child.

Gaining weight while being pregnant was normal, but after losing the last baby, it only led to further depression and much weight gain. She felt fat, overwhelmed, and lonely. She was slowly spiraling and no one noticed, for they'd only pitied her because of the losses. As time went on, Samantha's grief was like a deep wound that eventually healed and closed but whose terrible scar remained.

When Samantha would attend church services and saw other mothers with children, she'd purposely sit on another pew just to get away from them. She'd scan the pews for children and it had become so natural that no one noticed. If they'd accidentally sit by her, she'd leave to go the restroom only to sit elsewhere when returning.

In the evenings or summer days, when school was out and mothers would take their children shopping, Samantha knew too well those dates and times. She would just stay home those days just to keep from suffering such heart-aches. She would either shop early in the mornings or late at night if she had to.

When she and Russell would attend church services together, which was every blue moon, again she would examine the pews and purposely sit close to the front rows, never looking back at families or mothers with children on the other pews. Most families with children would sit closer to the back, and that was fine with her. No one ever noticed why and never questioned why.

Samantha seldom ate out in the evenings in fear of seeing families with their children. Again, it would be either early in the mornings or late at night or not at all, during the school year or summer months. Depression was all over Samantha and she tried to overcome it without drinking alcohol or turning to drugs. Little did Samantha know that further trouble was brewing ahead, one that nearly tipped the iceberg as the rug was about to be pulled out from beneath her.

A Lesson Learned

One day, Samantha decided to go shopping at the local mall. It was early in the morning and during the time when children were at school. She saw a little girl navigating the stairway. The little girl was approximately two years old. The little girl was alone as her mother waited at the bottom of the stairs for her. One by one, the little girl took the steps down to the lower level.

At first, when Samantha saw the little girl, she started to abruptly leave. But something told her to stay, for there was a lesson to be learned. Descending the stairs was this little girl's mission and she wanted to accomplish it. As her mother waited until the little girl stepped on the last step, her mother opened her arms widely in gratitude until the child had made it.

The lesson Samantha took away was that God is with us in every step we take. Whether we are ascending and things are going great in happy times or descending in times of trouble, pain, or sorrow, He's there with us, with wide open arms to happily embrace us. Samantha just smiled and thanked the Lord for the courage to stay and wait, and for the lesson He'd taught her from a simple child.

Chapter 12
It's Not Over

Russell, Russell, Russell

One Sunday morning, Samantha had begun to get dressed for church, while Russell seemed to be sleeping in as usual. It was very cloudy outside and thunder was roaring as the lightning flashed.

"Are you going to church this morning, baby?" asked Samantha.

"No, I'm not feeling well. You go ahead and I'll see you when you get back," replied Russell.

"Okay, baby," replied Samantha.

It had started to rain outside and once Samantha had gotten dressed, she attempted to get into her vehicle with her umbrella. The winds had broken her umbrella from the position of an 'n' to the position of a 'u.' Yet, she made it into her vehicle being slightly dampened from the rain as she headed to church. The winds were picking up even more and the rain was coming down in waves.

Samantha noticed that there weren't a lot of vehicles in the parking lot as normal. Samantha attempted to attend church services, but on this particular Sunday when she'd gotten to the front door, a notice explained that services were cancelled due to a tornado threat and bad weather. So, she decided to go back home to be safe and take care of her ailing husband.

Driving very slowly, Samantha finally made it home. She'd begun to drive up the driveway and parked her vehicle. She ran to the front door because of the wind and rain. Desperately trying to enter her home through the front door with her keys, the door did indeed open, but she'd noticed that a chair was blocking the pathway. Samantha wondered, *'why is a chair there when this had never occurred and it wasn't there when I'd left for church?'* Samantha now had to run and enter the residence through the side door instead. The rain had dampened her even more as she desperately turned the key. This door had a clear pathway, so she was finally inside her home.

She quietly had taken off her shoes and earrings. She headed toward the bedroom.

"Mmm... Mmmm... Mmmm!" Samantha heard moaning coming from her bedroom. At first, she figured Russell was snoring and laughed it off. Samantha continued toward the bedroom and opened the door. She found Russell in bed, but the covers had another large hump on the other side of him. Actually it was where she slept.

Suddenly, up raised another woman lying beside Russell in Samantha's spot. It was the same bed that she and Russell shared as husband and wife. Russell and the unknown woman were totally nude, sweaty, embarrassed, and shocked. Samantha was distraught, shocked, and taken back. She was perplexed and confused at first, but reality sank in. How could Russell do this to her after all she'd done for him, she thought. After all the hurt and pain she'd already endured by the loss of five children, how could he? Yet, sure enough, it was lying Russell in the flesh, in their bed, with a three-hundred-pound naked woman.

"Russell, get out. Both of you, get out. Get out!" screamed Samantha. "I don't ever want to see you again, Russell."

It had been all too clear of the annoying phone calls she'd been receiving. The phone calls that Russell denied ever knowing of its source were one and the same. It was all too clear now and God had revealed it to her, though not in the way she'd expected. Samantha wondered why this child would call and ask for his daddy. It was out of spite that the child's mother had put the child up to this mean act, Samantha figured. How could anyone do this to her, she'd ask herself.

It also had become abundantly clear as to why Russell would hardly attend church services with Samantha. Instead of taking this mistress to a cheap hotel, Russell used their secret bed instead. This was so disrespectful and dirty, Samantha felt. This was against everything she'd learned in the church about God and family, about husband and wife.

If you really want to know, Russell really wasn't the 'true' love of Samantha. She'd married Russell out of gratitude to his mother for taking her in. Yet, Samantha grew to love Russell because of his goodness, but love, no, infatuated she used to be. Samantha could have easily lived the rest of her life with Russell because he was indeed her husband that she'd felt God had given her, but not after this.

Russell packed up his belongings and walked toward the door. Samantha was crying and frustrated all the while. They argued back and forth about his lying and how their marriage was nothing but a lie. Russell had very little to say in this argument, for he was guilty as charged. Russell slowly walked out of the door, got into his vehicle, and left. Samantha watched him from the window with tears in her eyes, but he didn't see her.

A rollercoaster of emotions was what Samantha was feeling. She had feelings of numbness, disbelief, anger, guilt, sadness, depression, and rejection all at once. She already knew that the days and months ahead would be further filled with feelings of fatigue, trouble sleeping, sleeping alone, difficulty concentrating, loss of appetite or gaining of appetite, and frequent episodes of crying. She already had known the days ahead would be difficult because the finances would be less as well.

'So many trials and thorns,' Samantha thought to herself. She'd known women who'd had great husbands and many children in their household. Here, she was the result of a no-good husband, childless, and had scars from her youth. Samantha thought that if she'd worshipped God, life would be rosy and great. As she looked upon the outward appearance, it seemed that everyone else was doing fine except her.

The thorns and tribulations kept Samantha on her knees praying to God. Little did she know that it was where God had wanted her to be. Sure others had it better, but some had it worse. Others had little time for God and prayer, as they'd basked in their own happiness and had taken God for granted. God was with Samantha the entire time to carry her through the difficult days and nights. God can never use a prideful person, but delights in a humble person. Why so much pain, no one will ever know, but God was there. God is the same yesterday, today, and forever.

Samantha vowed never to trust a man again. She vowed that the only man she would ever trust again would be the Lord Jesus. Jesus had been there through all the thorns from day one, she'd felt.

Chapter 13
The Absent Youth

The Loss of Childhood

Oftentimes, Samantha would look back on her life as she reminisced. She wondered if she could have made better choices or if she'd been born into disaster. She would speak to other women to either get advice or give it, who may have been going through a difficult time themselves.

Samantha had a really close relationship with Jesus and because she'd been wounded so deeply, she avoided close relationships altogether. She feared being hurt more and chose not to even have a close friend. Her childhood was forever etched in her mind and the thought of the past had consumed a lot of her time.

Samantha

'Whenever I looked back at what has happened to me, all the abuse (emotional, physical, verbal, and mental, etc. in many assorted forms), one occurrence that always attacked my mind was this feeling of having my childhood stolen from me. I was never given an opportunity to have friends, engage in primary interests, or even be some of the corny stereotype teen with an attitude that you may see on TV. Not only did I feel this overbearing feeling of being wounded and scarred, but I also felt this feeling of anger. I was angry toward my abuser and those who'd allowed it to happen and anger at the overall society for not letting me be me. I was angry at myself for trying to 'fix' myself and failing miserably in the process.

To this day, for me, this is something I am still struggling to wrap my head around. My parents should have gotten help with their alcoholism. AAA wasn't available at that time, but their pastor could have stepped in, I felt. There weren't any 'step programs' for my parents to realize the stages of alcohol abuse they were in. We, my siblings, and I suffered the consequences of their affects. That bygone era has set in each and every one of us, especially me.'

Growing Up Early

Children, at least until they've reached the 'terrible teens stage,' are seen as playful, innocent, and childlike creatures in need of exceptional protection. Parents should be fiercely determined to keep their childhood a carefree 'golden age.' Many households are not receiving this kind of protection due to drug or alcohol abuse. When sexual abuse enters into the picture, it's a whole new set of problems.

Children in this day and time are expected to grow up into early adulthood. They are expected to understand their parent's problems and frustrations early on. Many would miss out at the chance to be childish, immature, and unafraid. Now it's two-career families or divorce that grows a child up earlier than usual. In some ways, growing up early can be a good thing and in many ways, it's not a good thing.

Much of Samantha's past was about struggling as a family. Birthdays really weren't celebrated with cake, ice cream, and gifts, but with just a 'happy birthday' in words only. There were bills to be paid and evictions to be taken care of. Many times, Samantha's family really couldn't celebrate birthdays and Christmas as a whole and she felt that her parents had again let her down in all areas of her life.

The Evening Russell Left

What determined Samantha's direction in life? She'd now lost five innocent babies and was now without a husband to tell her everything was going to be alright. She attempted to do the only thing she was familiar with. Samantha looked at her purse as it sat on the kitchen table. She went to her purse and opened it. Inside her purse were her car keys and wallet. She thought to herself:

Samantha

'I'm going to the liquor store for sure now. If anyone deserves a drink, it's me. I'm going to get sloppy drunk and come home and cry myself to sleep. That's what I'm going to do.'

Samantha began to pause for a moment, and she began to envision her mother's drunken face, a vision that had always haunted her. She also had visions of her mother's nonchalantness as she allowed her close relative to rape and molest her. She was now standing still as she was paused. She questioned herself if this would be the road she should take, a lifetime of being a drunken stupor. God entered into Samantha's mind, the God of 'peace and tranquility,' the God of 'everything was going to be alright,' the God of 'trust me,' the God of 'I'll never leave you nor forsake you,' the God of 'I've been here all alone, even during the times of rape,' and the God of 'I was even there with Baby Mitchell One to Five.'

After a sudden pause, Samantha began to fall on her knees right there in the living room, with the car keys in her hand. It was as though God entered into her spirits and now she had overwhelmingly chosen God instead of the drunken stupor. She cried and realized that since she was there on her knees, maybe she should pray earnestly. She falls in prostrated position and pours her heart out in prayer to God.

Samantha

'Dear Lord, what have I done to deserve this treatment? Are you that angry with me that I was rebellious against my mother? Do you hate me like I've hated my mother? Lord, I've lost five children and my husband has been having an affair behind my back for who knows how long. He's even disrespected our secret bed by bringing another woman in it. Are you angry with me, dear Lord? Why? Why? Why, Lord? Why? I'm sorry, Lord. I'll try more and more to forgive my mother. I'll try, but she did me so bad, Lord. She did me so bad. Help me to forgive her, Lord. Some days, I can forgive her while other days, it very hard. Help me, Lord.

Give me a good husband and a baby one day, Lord. I promise you that I'll treat my baby better than my mom treated me. I will never let anything happen to my baby. The doctors told me not to get pregnant again, but I trust you, Lord. I can do all things through Christ who strengthens me. I know you can strengthen me, Lord, please. Don't let me be an alcoholic like my mother, Lord, please.

Give me a good man one day, Lord. I promise I'll let the world know we are one in you. I'll serve you, Lord – me and my family. I'll serve you, please, Lord, please. Help me, Lord. Please help me.

Why did you let my close relative rape me, Lord, when I was only a baby. It hurt so badly, Lord. It hurt so badly. It hurt so badly. Lord, I need you. I need you, Lord. I need you, Jesus. Send your help to my thirsty soul. Fill me with your loving and holy spirit. Please open up the heavens and take control of my life. Don't let me suffer by being alone and discouraged because I've lost my children and husband.

How can I make it without my husband, oh, Lord? How? I can't do it alone. Please help me. Please help me, Lord. Please, please, please. I cry. How can I pay this house note, my car note, and how can I feed myself? How? How? How? Will I be hungry and put out on the streets like my parents? Please help me, Lord, please. Please, my dear Lord. In Jesus's name I pray. Amen.'

After slowly getting up from the prostrated position, Samantha wiped the tears from her eyes. She went into her bedroom and was going to lie down but thought what Russell had been doing there with this unknown woman. She took off all the sheets and pillowcases and threw them into the washer to be cleaned. She poured tons of bleach in the washer. Instead of lying on her bed, she went into the living room with another set of covers and headed for the couch. She sat down and began to lay down as she cried her heart out.

The Bible was on the coffee table nearby. Samantha picked it up, not knowing what to read or where to turn; she just opened it up and started searching. Samantha happened upon the book of Deuteronomy. She glanced down to Chapter Thirty-One. It said:

"Then Moses went out and spoke these words to all Israel: 2 'I am now a hundred and twenty years old and I am no longer able to lead you. The Lord has said to me, 'You shall not cross the Jordan.' The Lord, your God Himself, will cross over ahead of you. He will destroy these nations before you, and you will take possession of their land. Joshua also will crossover ahead of you as the Lord said. 4 And the Lord will do to them what He did to Sihon

101

and Og, the kings of the Amorites, whom He destroyed along with their land." [2]

Samantha paused for a moment to take in what she'd just read. Could it mean that since Moses was one hundred and twenty years, he was tired just like she was tired? Could it meant that Moses was tired of the Israelites complaining once they'd crossed the Red Sea and he was just frustrated like she was frustrated? What meaning did God have for her to learn from these verses?

Samantha realized that when God told Moses that He'd cross over ahead of him, it meant that God would go before her and take care of everything? Samantha almost decided to stop reading, but something kept telling her to keep going. After all, she had nothing else to do but sit and cry. Samantha further read:

5 "The Lord will deliver them to you, and you must do to them all that I have commanded you. 6. Be strong and courageous. Do not be afraid or terrified because of them, for the Lord, your God, goes with you; He will never leave you nor forsake you."[2]

"Be strong," God told Samantha, "and be courageous. Do not be afraid or terrified because of them." Somehow, she found strength in these verses. It meant for her not to worry because God would take care of all those who had hurt her, even her mother and close relative. She remembered being slapped in the face by her mother and kicked out of the house with nowhere to go. She felt her mother didn't care what could have happened to her, as she was sent out on the dark streets in the middle of a thunderstorm. God provided then and Samantha knew that God would provide now while in the midst of this thorny *storm*.

God said He would never leave her nor forsake her. Oh, how much strength did Samantha get just by happenstance upon these scriptures. Samantha smiled and was somehow at peace. She knew that if God did it then, He'll do it again and again. Samantha fell to her knees again in prayer:

'Lord, I thank you for your Word in this time of my hurt and prickly pain. I know you'll be with me through this difficult time in my life. Lead me, Lord.

Please, lead me. Jesus, my Jesus, Your love is all that I need. Not my mother's, not my father's, and not my husband's love. Help me. Oh Lord, I believe. Please help my unbelief. Your love is all that I need. Thank you, Jesus, for your guidance and your mercy. Thank you for loving me when no one else would. In your name, Jesus, I pray. Amen.'

Lifting herself from the floor, she lay back down on the couch. Her eyes were heavy from all the crying. Samantha fell asleep with tears running down her face. She was at peace now and she slept for hours.

Chapter 14
Forgiveness

Athena Becomes Ill

As years passed, Athena, Samantha's mother, had started to forget simple things around the house. Mrs. Athena was beginning to be in a pitiful state. Samantha still resented her mother for the past, but she cared about her wellbeing. After all, she was her mother. Samantha's other siblings had still held in some resentment toward Mrs. Athena and they'd refused to care for her. Being a believer of Jesus Christ, Samantha had to put her resentment aside for Christ's sake and take care of her mother. It seemed hard at first. However, it had become easier over time. *'What would Jesus do?'* as the saying goes, was the pattern Samantha had to take. Jesus would have forgiven those who'd wronged him, who'd spat in his face, who'd plucked out the hairs of his beard, who'd thrown rocks at him, who'd whipped him for no reason, and for sinners he'd died, like me and you who sin every day. If Jesus could do it, Samantha had to try and not hold her hate inside that was becoming self-destructive.

Samantha had taken her mother to the doctor's office where she'd learned that she was diagnosed with dementia. It was not known how long Mrs. Athena had the disease, but one thing was for sure; she couldn't handle her everyday task alone. Research has shown that:

'The disease known as Alzheimer's is considered a type of cerebrum disease, just as coronary artery disease is in the category of heart disease. It is also a degenerative disease, implying that it becomes atrocious with time. Alzheimer's disease has been assessed to begin twenty years or more prior to the evidence arise, with small alterations in the brain that are unobserved to

the person impacted. Exclusively after years of brain alterations do individuals experience distinctive danger signs such as memory displacement and speech difficulties. Evidences arise because nerve cells (neurons) in a percentage of the brain required in intelligence, knowledge, and recollection (cognitive function) become devastated or blighted. Individuals who are unremarkable live with Alzheimer's manifestations for years. After a while, manifestations have a tendency to intensify and start impeding with the individuals' potential to accomplish everyday interest. By then, the person is said to have dementia that is linked to the Alzheimer's disease, or Alzheimer's Dementia.'

Samantha

'After years of dealing with someone who was incapable of showing me any respect or love, I can say that I have finally broken free from my mother's bondage. After all of these years, I can finally be the person who I want to be. It was as if I had just now begun to live. I will continue to write about my experiences as a child; hopefully, what I have been through will help others who are going through similar circumstances. I now know that a new beginning is possible no matter what life had thrown my way.'

Growing up in life with a mother that seemed to hate you was very difficult, especially as a child, Samantha said. The weight that had been carried upon her shoulders had been very heavy at times. Many tears were shed even after Samantha had gotten grown. Secret tears were what she'd shed, as her heart pounded with hate and anxiety.

Yet, Mrs. Athena was becoming sicker by the day. One of Samantha's older brothers would try to help take care of Athena until he'd had a heart attack himself and was barely able to take care of himself. No other of Athena's children would step up to the challenge. So, Samantha had made it up in her mind that she would try to take care of her mother better than she'd taken care of her.

When Samantha first started to take care of her mother, she'd felt bitter inside. She had to rearrange her own lifestyle as her mother's disease had progressed, something her mother, Mrs. Athena, never seemed to do when Samantha was small. Sometimes, Samantha would temporarily be angry with God, but she prayed about it. God revealed to her in her heart of how she'd been selfish for most of life after she'd become an adult. Tears began to well in her eyes as she confessed. Even though her mother never hugged, kissed, or told her she loved her, God helped Samantha to see things differently. Samantha was living in the past and not from day to day. She'd attend church services for her and not for the praise and worship of Jesus Christ alone. Samantha realized that God pours out His love for her because His mercies are new every morning. Everyday, she lives is a new day in which she can draw closer to and in a direction that defines her eternity. She should not be content with the things of this world, but in God's continual and unchanging mercy; His saving grace. From that day forward, Samantha did everything for her mother out of love for Jesus. Caring for Samantha's mother had become the greatest privilege of her life.

Sometimes, God had answered Samantha's prayers not by giving her what she'd wanted but by challenging her to change. Samantha forgave Athena for the beatings, slaps in the face, adulterous relationships, alcoholic binges, lack of food, putting her out of the house at age fifteen, and much, much more.

Samantha sought the Lord and heeded to His advice as she continued to read His Word. She read in the Book of Matthew 6:12-15:

"And forgive us our debts, as we also have forgiven our debtors. And lead us not into temptation, but deliver us from the evil one." [2]

Samantha

'For if you forgive other people when they sin against you, our heavenly Father will also forgive us when we've sinned. But if you do not forgive others their sins, our Father will not forgive our sins. It bears repetition because sometimes we don't think we've sinned. The truth of the matter is we do sin every day, knowingly and unknowingly.'

Remembering her own sins of being rebellious toward her mother, Samantha used to struggle when it came to forgiveness. Samantha would often read Isaiah 55:7:

"Let the wicked forsake their ways and the unrighteous their thoughts. Let them turn to the LORD, and He will have mercy on them, and to our God, for He will freely pardon." [2]

Hoping that her mother was saved and forgiven by God, one day, while caring for her mother, she noticed that her mother had soiled her pants and needed cleaning. Samantha washed the filth off her mother and cleaned her up. While doing so, her mother spoke,

"I'm... so, so– I'm sorry for how I treated you, Samantha," said Athena. Samantha paused. Moments later, Samantha began to speak.

"That's okay, Momma," said Samantha as tears were welled up in both of their eyes. The room had become very quiet and still as Samantha began to hum a hymn. Athena faintly joined her.

"Mamma, are you saved?" asked Samantha.

"What do you mean?" asked Athena.

"Do you believe that God is the Lord of your life and Jesus died on the cross for our sins?"

"Yeah, I think so," replied Athena.

"Would you repeat after me then, Momma?" asked Samantha.

"Yeah," Athena faintly answered as though she was surprised that the one child she'd mistreated the most cared enough about whether she'd enter into heaven or hell.

"Repeat after me, Momma," advised Samantha as Athena did just that.

"Dear Lord Jesus,

Thank you for dying on the cross for my sins. Please forgive me for all the sins I've committed, Lord Jesus. Come into my life. I receive you as my Lord and Savior. Now, help me to live for you the rest of this life. In the name of Jesus, I pray. Amen."

"Does that mean that I'm good now, Sam?" asked Athena.

"You're good, Mamma. You're good. You're good now," replied Samantha as she smiled toward her mother's wondering face. Mrs. Athena slowly arose from her sick bed as she reached her arms out to hug Samantha. Samantha was confused at first because she'd never reached out to hug her before, never. It seemed awkward and very unusual to see this sight from her mother. Samantha slowly hugged her mother back for the first time. Then, they embraced for a long time as tears welled up in Samantha's eyes. Samantha didn't think that her mother ever knew what that hug meant to her, as Mrs. Athena had a smile on her face while hugging her. Yet, to Samantha it meant the world, as she'd never known the hug of a mother. It felt so good inside to Samantha. It softened the blows from the past as the forgiving process was really starting to unfold.

It seemed that Athena knew deep down that she wasn't a good mother, especially to Samantha. Years and years of battling her mother's hatefulness and cruelness toward Samantha wouldn't be totally forgotten with a simple prayer, as it would take some time going forward to soften the scars that were so dwelt within from the piercingly thorns. The prayers did help and one day, the forgiveness would be completed, as prayer was only the start.

Unselfish Samantha had placed a large grimace on Athena's face. Samantha could see it all for herself that she'd made a difference in her mother's life when no one else cared enough. All the adultery and all the selfishness that Athena had done were now forgiven and she wanted to live right from that day on. The very person that Athena mistreated in the past was the very one who had to take care of her when she'd become sick. Athena couldn't pick up the wasted spilled milk, but she could use the remaining milk that was left to live a new life of love without looking back at the many mishaps.

Unfortunately, a few months later, Athena's Alzheimer's disease had become much worse and it was too much for Samantha to care for her at home. Athena needed around-the-clock care, so Samantha placed her in a nursing home. Samantha visits her mother to this day as Athena has had good days and bad days. Samantha sure couldn't hurt Ms. Athena with resentment or harsh words now if she'd wanted to, so why try? Now, sometimes Ms. Athena remembers who Samantha is and sometimes she doesn't. Athena doesn't remember the past mishaps even if Samantha or anyone else were to try to bring them to her recollection.

It's funny. Athena now doesn't remember mistreating Samantha because of the Alzheimer's disease. So, why should Samantha remember the past herself? She would only be hurting the one that mattered. Samantha had to move forward and keep looking forward. It was the only good thing that came out of Athena's disease, forgetting the past mistakes.

Chapter 15
Samantha Moves on

Time for a Change

Samantha tried to move on with her life, for she and Russell were now divorced. She discovered from a friend that the lady that Russell was having an affair with had several fatherless children and none were actually Russell's. Samantha now knew that the adulteress would just call her house only to antagonize her because she wanted Russell as her own.

Samantha

'*Being able to talk about my circumstances and hardships really has helped me through it. The more people I shared my miscarriages, sexual assaults, and my first adulterous husband with, the more I felt strong. I didn't know that there were so many women who were going through the same thing as me. Of course, talking doesn't really erase what has happened, but it helps to know you're not alone*'.

A Controlling Marriage

Russell had been very controlling toward Samantha. In hindsight, she realized it and promised herself it must not be repeated going forward. Controlling behavior from a spouse knew no boundaries. People of any age, gender, sexual orientation, or socioeconomic status can be in controlling relationships, playing either role.

Many of us envision a possessive partner as one who openly denigrates everyone in their way, is physically confrontational, or persistently makes conspicuous threats or ultimatums. We often have impressions of the grumpy tyrant who deprecates every server he or she engages with or orders their significant other on how to dress from top to bottom and, while those indicators are certainly irritating, there are many supplementary indications that might shed light quite distinctly.

Dianna

'Individuals that have restrictions on another utilize a whole arsenal of implements in order to have ascendancy over their partners. It doesn't matter if they or their significant other comprehend what's occurring or not. Occasionally, the temperamental influence is complicated enough that the individual who is being dominated really is convinced that they themselves are the offender or that they are exceptionally fortunate that their dominating partner 'puts up' with them. Nonetheless, if the dominating abuse leads to more turbulent emotional or physical mistreatment or not, it is not a wholesome environment.'

Here are some additional clues that your partner may be controlling. I would encourage you to research these clues if you want further answers.

- *Persistent condemnation, even over small matters*
- *Incapability or reluctance to ever hear your side of the story*
- *Forcing you toward harmful conduct, like addictions and substance abuse*
- *Frustrating your educational or educational objectives by allowing you to doubt yourself*
- *Masked or undisguised threats against themselves or you*
- *Manufacturing welcoming/warmhearted/desirability condition*
- *An exaggerated scorecard*
- *Using remorse as a means to control*
- *Getting you so exhausted of controversial disagreements that you'll change your mind*
- *Making you feel depreciated for long-held opinions*
- *Separating you from loved ones*
- *Constructing a financial obligation you're indebted to*
- *Surveillance, prying, or requiring consistent communication*

- *Overactive enviousness, allegation, or obsession*
- *Not regarding your space for self-solitariness*
- *Assuming you're blameworthy until proven innocent*
- *Making you feel underserving of them*
- *Making fun or scoffing that has an uneasy undertone*
- *Sexual communications that feel distressing subsequently*

It Was Time to Move On

It was time for Samantha to move on, and because Russell had been so controlling throughout their marriage, she felt free as a bird. Yet, she'd missed the nurturing of a husband and the feeling of being in a relationship. Moreover, now she was able to go out with girlfriends and not worry about being back home at a certain time. She didn't have to rush back to cook for Russell and she could dress the way she wanted and put whatever kind of hair she wanted on her head. It felt strange at first, but soon she could be the person she always wanted to be.

Going to college was something Samantha had always wanted to do as well. So, she picked up some college hours in the *behavior and medical field*, something she could never do before. She could stay as long as she wanted at church, something else she couldn't do before because Russell would always be in such a rush to get home and hit the streets, without her that is.

Moreover, after a while, Samantha had settled into her new life, but oftentimes she'd become lonely because she'd always had someone to talk to, care for, and she'd missed being married, not the controlling marriage she'd once had, but just the company of marriage. Besides, she'd made it up in her mind that she was not getting married again, partly because of the controlling issues and also the heartaches and thorns that sometimes came with it. Yet, at a low moment, she happened upon someone.

Samantha's Infatuation

One day, Samantha was at her mother's house, taking care of her mother's business and concerns because she was in a nursing home. The telephone rang.

"Hello," said Samantha.

"Hello, uh, may I speak to Samuel?" asked the caller.

"Samuel," replied Samantha.

"Yes," said the caller.

"I'm sorry, there is no Samuel here. You must have the wrong number," said Samantha.

"Okay, thank you," said the unknown caller.

"You're welcome," Samantha responded. Samantha went on to take care of some business matters of her mother. She also had done some much-needed cleaning and dusting around the house when the telephone rang again.

"Hello," said Samantha.

"Hello," said the caller. Samantha recognized the caller as the person who'd just called asking for an unknown person by the name of Samuel. He continued to speak.

"I'm gonna come by your house to see you," said the caller.

"I beg your pardon?" responded Samantha.

"I'm gonna come by your house to see you in just a little while," said the caller.

"Sir, you don't know who I am or where I live," replied Samantha.

"I bet I do know where you live and I'll be right over," said the caller. Rather than entertain strangers or stalkers, Samantha just hung up the telephone.

After finishing up the dusting at her mom's house, Samantha had gone outside to see if there was anything her mother needed done there. She walked over to the side of the house and had begun to pick up the rake when an unknown gentleman approached her. He was a nice-looking guy and didn't seem to want to do her any harm, but Samantha had her guards up.

"See, I told you I know where you live," said the stranger.

"Okay," said Samantha in a shocked and fearful way.

"Actually, your cousin Albert gave me your phone number and told me where you stayed," said the stranger. "My name is Martin and I've been asking your cousin about you for a while," said the stranger.

"Oh, okay. I'm Samantha." The guy stuttered when he spoke, but he had a kind demeanor and that had gotten Samantha's attention.

"You're pretty," Martin said. This warmed Samantha's heart that someone felt she was pretty.

"Thank you," Samantha responded.

Samantha

Samantha explained she and Martin dated for a while, but she was never in love with Martin. It was that he'd caught her at a moment when she was very lonely. After her divorce was final with Russell, Samantha and Martin began a relationship. Dating was something she'd never thought she'd do again, but sometimes loneliness and depression will make you change your mind.

Thinking about transitioning?

Dianna

'During the time an individual ponders whether to get married or proceed to date, inquiring about the positives and negatives of either alternative will likely ensue. The individual may converge on the liberation that advances with dating brings, or they may enjoy the concept that matrimony bestows a kind of protection from the external sphere as well as a secure location to be themselves. Engagements dispense the advantageous one to construct a reliable infrastructure before engaging into the marriage responsibility. It also presents less steadiness in their liaison. Many of those that are in love with the notion of marriage feel that it lowers the risk of depression, and the communion also may have repercussions in monetary impediments, exclusively if a pair marries at an inexperienced age.'

Screening Your Mate

Back then, when Samantha and Martin were dating, there weren't a lot of places someone could go to research an individual's background that they were interested in dating or marrying. Samantha wants people to know that some things if had she'd known then, she would have never dated until she'd first researched their background. There were several questions that needed to be asked before getting into a relationship and the answers could have saved her a lot of thorny heartaches. Samantha shares this information because she didn't have it at that time. There are a few questions she says you should ask before you get into a relationship or get married, and they are below:

Question #1: *What portion of our revenue am I willing to consume to invest and maintain our residence on an annual or monthly arrangement?*

Question #2: *Who will be dependable for retaining our residence and landscaping? Are we dissimilar in our necessities for organization and cleanliness?*

Question #3: *As a combination, how many monetary funds do we obtain together? Presently? In two years? In six years? Fifteen? Between the two of us, who is accountable for which percentage? Presently? In two years? Six? Fifteen?*

Question #4: *What is our concluding monetary plan concerning yearly earnings, and when do we foresee attaining it? Consider your measures, virtues, and endeavors.*

Question #5: *What are our brackets of expenditures (clothing, travel, insurance, and rent)? How much do we disburse presently and in future, in each respective bracket? What amount are we allowed to spend?*

Question #6: *What is the time allotted that each of us will spend at work, and what hours of the day do we spend at work? Should we work separate shifts or the same? Do we prefer to work mornings or evenings?*

Question #7: *Under what circumstances should one of us not work? For what reasons?*

Question #8: *What are our aspirations? Is it a comfortable level of enthusiasm for both parties?*

Question #9: *What are our sexual comfort zones, whether giving or receiving? When performing intercourse, does each feel their love for the other?*

Question #10: *Do we both feel we are pleased with the frequency of our affection for each other? Are we able to cope when our satisfying levels of intercourse aren't met, whether it's a little, whether it's a lot, or whether it's weekly, monthly, or yearly?*

Question #11: *Should we eat our meals together or not? Discuss each meal together. Who is accountable for the grocery shopping? Of the two of us, who should prepare which meal? Discuss who should clean up after each meal.*

Question #12: *How does each undertake health issues and how they are approached? What tendencies or concerns does each have about habits, such as poor diets, smoking, drinking, or dieting?*

Question #13: *How does each fit in when it comes to the other's family life? When it comes to visiting or socializing, how often should we allocate to it? Should out-of-town relatives stay for an extended period of time?*

Question #14: *When we start a family, should the child's grandparents play an instrumental part in their lives? Who should and who shouldn't?*

Question #15: *If both decide to start a family, when is the best time? How many children should we have? Is having children important? Why or why not?*

Question #16: *Talk about how having children will change the household function. Discuss how once children enter the picture, then all questions mentioned are subject to change and so will their answers.*

Question #17: *Discuss your present friends, no matter how many. Once married, should we cut back on socializing when it seems the other is overwhelmed or even dissatisfied or neglected?*

Question #18: *What are each other's involvements for encouraging or preserving friendships outside our relationship?*

Question #19: *Is there a shared religion? Do we belong to a temple, sanctuary, mosque, or synagogue? If the answer is no, what faith relationship would we benefit from such a membership?*

Question #20: *What is our individual ecclesiastical observance? What times should be acceptably allocated to the other party? Is each able to revere the other's faith choice?*

Samantha thought she had screened Martin well enough, but some things were so hidden that even a psychiatrist wouldn't have been able to figure out. Plus, over three-fourth of the questions above weren't asked while she and Martin dated. It was more or less *'let's-get-married'* and *'let's-get-a-house-together.'* Please ask these questions, and if the answers don't seem right to you, rethink your commitment.

There are so many websites you can go to and do a background check on a person and the pros about internet are just the tip of the iceberg when it comes to finding personal information about someone. Many websites will give you a background-check engine that's simple and easy. With just a few clicks of your mouse, you can find detailed and explicit information that's not readily available through a standard search engine.

There is some information on the web and organizations where you will be able to check someone's entire history.

Dianna

'Although some internet sites can show deeply surprisingly criminal documents, I've really been astonished by just how feasible it is as an ordinary tool. I've browsed the internet to look up phone numbers, birthdates, assets, estimated income levels, and addresses. One time, I looked up a known serial killer who'd confessed to several murders. I was surprised to find that in his background profile, the things listed were downright petrifying. This killer's profile came up when I checked his background report, and baby, let me tell you, I, as a veteran police officer, was horrified. He precisely left critiques on shovels, knives, and had deliberated on how he'd use them in the homicides. I could not believe this stuff won on the internet. But then again, why wouldn't it be? Everything else is.'

Samantha's Second Marriage

After dating for about a year, Samantha and Martin decided to tie the knot, for she thought she'd known him well enough. It was wedding bells for Samantha again. She and Martin dated a while after her divorce was final from Russell. She'd felt Martin was her soul mate. He was secure, kind, and unlike Russell; he wasn't controlling.

They'd settled down into their own routine after the honeymoon. Samantha continued to work and Martin worked as well. It seemed as if things were going well. However, cracks later had begun to show.

Soon, Samantha noticed that Martin was changing or better yet, the real Martin was about to come out. She said, *"Martin had a very bad disposition about himself."* She further said that:

Samantha

'One day I would come home and Martin would be very jolly, while other days he acted like he was ready to bite my head off. I never knew what to expect from Martin. I wished these tools were available back then or I had asked others in his inner circle or even my cousin Albert more about him. I would have run as fast as I could away from him. I thought to myself, 'What have I gotten myself into?' First of all, he stuttered more and more like crazy, and second, he was an undiagnosed bipolar patient. Lord, what have I gotten myself into?

A Day of Surprises

One day, Samantha and a good friend, whose husband was a police officer, were outside just enjoying the food and sunshine on their patio. Martin was at work and it was just her and the couple that were there socializing.

"How's your marriage to Martin?" asked the police officer.

"It's okay, much better than the last," Samantha laughed.

"You know he's a murderer," said the police officer.

"What?!" Samantha surprisingly screamed. Her heart began to race heavily and her palms became sweaty. She had sweat dripping down her face just that quickly and she tried to get her composure.

"Yeah," said the officer.

"Murderer... Who did he murder?" asked Samantha.

"One of his girlfriends," the officer responded.

"Why didn't you tell me this before I married him?" asked Samantha.

"Well, it wasn't my business," said the officer.

"Wow," Samantha said.

"Well, if you would have come up dead, we would have known who did it," said the officer. Samantha was flabbergasted.

Samantha Was on a Mission

Samantha left the couple's residence abruptly and headed straight to the courthouse. While driving, her mind was wondering ninety miles to nothing. She kept thinking to herself, 'What if this man kills me?' and 'What if he chokes me to death in my sleep?' Her mind was racing.

Samantha

'Why didn't anyone tell me about Martin? Surely, the police officer told his wife, who was my good friend. At least I thought she was. Why did people allow me to marry this man if he'd killed someone? If I find out that Martin did kill someone, what was to stop him from killing me? Lord, after all I've gone through, why would you allow this to happen to me? I haven't wronged anybody, but bad always comes to me, Lord. Please don't let this be true, please, Lord.'

The Courthouse

Samantha arrived at the courthouse. She began to walk up the courthouse stairs, talking to herself silently along the way. She gave the clerk the information about her husband. The clerk did indeed find a report about the incident. Samantha paid for the report and looked over it as she walked out of the courthouse. She was about to run into something and decided to read it in a quiet place outside, like a park bench. She couldn't wait to read it at home, for she 'must know' now if the facts were correct and the circumstances surrounding it.

The Report

Samantha discovered from the report that a few years ago, her husband Martin, was seeing a young lady. They liked each other, but the relationship was new and not based on true love, just infatuation. One day, the young lady approached Martin and asked him if he wanted to do a *'threesome.'* Being surprised at the request, Martin agreed. The couple had driven around and found the other willing lady for the *'threesome'* and picked her up from a street corner. The three of them headed to a nearby secluded location in the vehicle, chitchatting along the way.

They parked in a private area and the three began to start heavy petting, kissing, and fondling one another. Martin kissed and fondled his girlfriend while the other unknown lady fondled him and his private parts. After a while, Martin began to kiss the unknown lady. The girlfriend began to fondle Martin more. Then, the unknown lady began to give Martin oral sex. Martin was really enjoying it and was moved by this transaction. His girlfriend was kissing him all the while.

Then it was time for the Martin to fondle the unknown lady. He started with the breast area and moved his hands down toward the private area. He felt a hump. He slowly stopped fondling. He felt the private part of the unknown lady again and the hump was still there. He stopped abruptly and felt a third time and that was when he realized that it was a man that had been dressed in women's clothing.

Martin got violently angry. He cursed the two companions out and pulled out a knife and started to stab the girlfriend, while the unknown male jumped out of the vehicle and ran fast. The unknown male ran to call the police because a knife was involved. After about five or so minutes later, the police showed up.

Police Investigation

After police investigated the incident, Martin was arrested. The transcript Samantha read was different from the police report she'd also gotten. Samantha had taken her time and read it over and over again. While in jail, Martin was advised by the detectives' report that the girlfriend he stabbed had died and the charges would be upgraded to murder instead of aggravated battery. The detectives asked Martin a series of questions pertaining to the incident. Martin seemed nonchalant about the entire ordeal the report advised.

After further reading the transcript, Samantha learned that Martin ultimately spent very little time in jail and she knew that his family was the reason. Samantha knew that Martin's family consisted of working-class people and probably had gotten a good lawyer.

After it was all said and done, Martin spent one year in jail. It was probably the reason for his nonchalance. Martin felt that he could commit murder anytime and his family would get him off.

There, Samantha sat as she placed the police report and transcript down on her lap. She thought to herself:

Samantha

'Oh my Goodness! It's true. Martin did kill someone. Martin did commit murder and got off because of his family. He wined and dined me and talked me into marrying him. I fell for it. I fell for it. I wonder why God allowed me to marry this crazy, murderous man. If I stay with him any longer, he may kill

me. I know at times I'd told the Lord I didn't want to live, especially when I was a young girl going through the raping and abuse by my close relative. I even thought about not living especially when I'd lost my babies. I really didn't mean it and I ain't ready to die just yet. I ain't ready for Martin to kill me either.'

Samantha headed home to confront Martin. She had to be careful not to set him off. She feared he may get angry and do the same to her as he'd done to his girlfriend. She feared that he would get off again and probably spend less than a year in jail because it was her, and the luck she'd been having lately wasn't really that good. She knew the police would arrest Martin, but he would probably get off again just as he did before.

Martin never revealed this information to Samantha before until she confronted him. There would neither be quarreling nor fighting during this conversation, for Samantha knew better. Samantha left him abruptly as she packed her bags and headed somewhere to seek shelter. The couple soon divorced, and again, Samantha vowed not to ever trust a man with her life and love and not to ever marry again.

Chapter 16
Lessons Learned

Is the Third Marriage a Charm?

Months and years had passed and it was lonely time again for Samantha. She had now divorced the adulterer and the murderer. Making sure she did not repeat the same mistakes, she vowed to be single and would not be looking for a mate, period. Jesus Christ would be her mate and He was enough for her.

Contentment Versus Marriage

Samantha was being content with her singleness. She didn't want to make any more mistakes. She figured that if the Good Lord wanted her to marry again, He'd have to place him at her doorstep, for she sure was not looking for him. She prayed through her loneliness and it did indeed pass.

Even though her first marriage was clearly out of obligation, she wondered if she really, really had to marry Russell. Had her mother-in-law been pressuring her into marrying her son because no one else would? Was he really ready to get married or at least marry her? She had more questions than answers, but one thing was for sure; she could not change her past.

Then there was Martin, the sweet-talker. Samantha really thought she loved Martin, not at first but as time went on. She questioned if it was true love or another one of her infatuations. Did she screen Martin like she should have or did she just marry him out of wanting so dearly to be loved? She needed to remember things going forward, if none other than to help someone else who may be undecided about their relationship.

There are some tips below that Samantha wanted to share with those who may be approaching marriage for more than the second time. Even though she didn't necessarily face some of these issues, she hoped the expert opinions will help others in whatever kind of relationship they may be facing. You may or may not see yourself in all thirteen tips, but one or two may hit home.

Dianna

'They say the third time may be the charm because after feeling like a two-time loser, it becomes more laborious to keep accusing the other person completely. Another familiar saying is, "Have an unsuccessful matrimony once. <u>Shame</u> on you. Have an unsuccessful matrimony twice. Shame on me." As we age, just being tired of always fighting is an admissible resolution to quarreling. Moreover, when you are younger, that seems to be no avoiding that consumed within us to compromise or resolve. By then, you're on a third matrimony and you've gone from believing you're indestructible to wanting to make it to the finish line of life with tranquility.

There are many individuals who will not remarry for the third time. I have a friend like that. She just didn't want to be like Elizabeth Taylor who'd been married eight or nine times without remorse. For the many individuals that do marry for the third-plus times, there are usually patterns they have acquired that helped their third marriage to triumph. They only wished they'd known it during the first and second times before'.

Patterns of a Thriving and Vigorous Third Marriage

1. **Communicating 'with' as an alternate of 'at' your partner.** *Allow their 'body expressions' to be your guide. Communicating at someone only makes the other tense up. Yet, when you're talking to them, they'll more than likely feel more stress-free.*
2. **Fine-tune in – as an alternative of fine-tuning out – to what your partner is communicating.** *Whether you're interested in their conversation or not, remember that every word your partner is saying is important. Don't allow your mind to wonder as though their words are insignificant.*
3. **Be mindful to thank your partner.** *Not being thoughtful, considerate, or appreciative toward your spouse when they themselves are just*

that toward you makes them feel undervalued and like an idiot for caring about you.

4. **Apologizing often as opposed to becoming defensive.** When you make a mistake, the sooner you apologize with sincerity, the sooner your partner can stop begrudging you.

5. **Follow through with your apology.** An apology helps in so many ways, one being that it buys you another opportunity. Yet, continually making the same mistakes makes your frequent apologies null and void.

6. **Being prompt.** Repeatedly allowing your partner to wait is very conceited and egotistical.

7. **Do not always jump to conclusions.** Don't assume you always know your partner's feelings. First get all the facts. Otherwise, you'll push them away and they'll resent you in the long run.

8. **Are you always playing the victim?** This conduct will not only accuse your spouse of always distressing you, but it will add insult to injury by insinuating that it's done intentionally, and that is not always the case.

9. **Are you insinuating your partner is always wrong?** Accept and realize that it takes two to dance. Yes, you too make mistakes. Stop blaming your partner for every mistake made.

10. **When your partner isn't around, talk well of them to others.** Don't talk bad about your spouse to others. It seems like you're keeping secrets from them and shows how little you revere them.

11. **Start making ground rules when issues regarding difference of opinions arise.** Agreeing with your partner not to use certain words like 'always' or 'never' can become insulting or have the ability of using unremittingly allegations that make each do a self-check when pointed out. Disagreements are normal but the many words can deteriorate the heart and get to a point where vicious words or measures can't be replayed or forgotten.

12. **Realizing once is not enough.** If you don't practice the measures above and not allow a self-check, you'll degenerate into bad mannerisms and you'll be ridiculing your partner. Don't fool yourself. If you're not committed to your marriage or your partner,

guess what? They can see right through your fake and halfhearted efforts.

13. What did Samantha do wrong in her other two marriages? *First of all, she didn't seek professional help for her abused past. Second, she'd lived for someone else and not taking care of the thorns that had pricked her so deeply. She'd longed for love that her parents were incapable of providing.*

Dianna

'Past statistics and research have shown that in the United States, fifty percent of first marriages, sixty-seven percent of second, and seventy-three percent of third marriages end in <u>divorce</u>. There are many reasons for this advancement of escalating <u>divorce percentages.</u> Hypotheses are plentiful. One ordinary justification is that a notable quantity of individuals infiltrates a second or third marriage on the 'ricochet' of a first or second divorce. Frequently, the individuals affected are <u>defenseless</u>, not allowing ample time to convalesce from their last relationship, a divorce, or to get their previous business or feelings straight before taking their pledge to another <u>again</u>. When entering into another marriage without internalizing the lessons learned from the previous, an individual may not have enough time to process their own mistakes. The individual may be liable to repeat their errors, making them gullible to indistinguishable encounters. One thing they will succeed at, and that is an additional disintegrated marriage, whatever the number may be.

Traditional prudence tells us that those who don't learn history are destined to replicate it. Ask yourself. Why are these marriages so much more likely to be unsuccessful? One feature by itself does not explain for such soaring percentages of second and third marriages.'

Chapter 17
A Wiser Samantha

Wisdom

Samantha was the wiser now, with two failed marriages and enough heart-aching, thorny experiences to give advice to everyone in the U.S. She was definitely not ready to date, let alone get remarried. Too many failed roads and too many bad choices she had made, some of them not her own accord.

There was a new program in town that helped the senior citizens of Shreveport have a better quality of life. Samantha's other siblings were slowly helping out with their mother at the nursing home even though Athena doesn't remember them because of the Alzheimer's disease. Samantha decided to work for this program and thought this would help her through the dark days of life, especially the lonely and depressive ones. There were senior programs that would help with:

- *Caregiver Recess*
- *Caregiver Suggestions and Counseling*
- *Insurance Waivers*
- *Adult Safekeeping Services and Elder Abuse*
- *Prevention*
- *Legal Aid*
- *Errand, Chore, and Homemaker Support*
- *State Health Insurance Assistance Plan of Action*
- *Senior Companion and Friendly Visitor Programs*
- *Transit Services*
- *Self-Directed Care Options*

- *Nourishment Counseling*
- *Senior Career and Employment*
- *Congregate and Home Delivered Meals*
- *Senior Accommodations and Housing Assistance*
- *Supplemental Nutrition*
- *Prescription Assistance Program*
- *Senior Housing Quarters and Apartments*

If you are a senior or know a senior in need of the above services, please contact your nearest state agency for details. Now that Samantha's dad was deceased and her mother was in a nursing home, this would give her a chance to help those elderly persons who would welcome her assistance to have a better quality of life.

Samantha applied and was fortunate to get a job working for a senator's wife's elderly aunt. 'Mamma Lottie' was her nickname. Samantha would take Mamma Lottie out to eat and help her run much-needed errands that she may have had. The job was rewarding and simple for Samantha.

By now, Shreveport and Bossier City, Louisiana, have six casinos in town. Each has a buffet that's out of this world. Every Thursday, Mamma Lottie loved to go to the 'Isle of Capri Casino,' to eat their buffet because it was free on certain days for seniors. Mamma Lottie didn't want the senator or her niece to know about the casino eatings, for it would be hers and Samantha's secret.

One day, while eating at the buffet, a nice gentleman who worked at the casino as a bartender kept eyeing Samantha, but she paid him no attention, of course. What Samantha did notice about the gentleman was that he always seemed happy and jovial. But fool Samantha once, shame on you. Fool her twice, shame on her. She was not going to let a jovial, whoever, sweet-talk his way into her life, not after what she'd been through.

The bartender found the courage one day to approach Samantha.

"You look like you're upset or angry all the time," said the unknown bartender. Samantha had been dealt a terrible blow throughout her life but didn't realize the anger and harshness was showing on her face.

"I'm okay," replied Samantha. She wasn't going to lead this man on in no shape, form, or fashion.

"You're pretty," said the bartender.

"Mhhmmm," replied Samantha, for she was not interested in his conversations or anything else and because she'd also heard those lines before. She thought to herself, *'Another sweet-talker.'*

The bartender kept talking as Samantha and Mamma Lottie continued on eating. After he left, Samantha never looked back, but the bartender did indeed look back at her. After eating, Samantha and Mamma Lottie got up and left the casino buffet.

"That was a nice young man, Samantha," said Mamma Lottie.

"He's alright," replied Samantha.

"Don't you like him, baby? He's handsome and sweet," asked Mamma Lottie.

"He's alright, Mamma Lottie," Samantha replied.

After about the fourth time of Mamma Lottie and Samantha's eating every Thursday at the Isle of Capri buffet, this young man kept trying to get Samantha's attention. It was as if he couldn't wait for Thursdays to come around just so he could see her. He kept easing his way over to Samantha to make her smile and ultimately laugh at his corny jokes, but Samantha was not bulging. This man worked at a bar, for God's sake. That was a strike against him already. She'd known too well from her past experiences with her parents what alcohol could and would do to a person and she wanted no part of it. *'He may actually drive me to drinking instead,'* Samantha thought to herself.

On one particular Thursday, this unknown bartender tried to make conversation with Samantha to no avail. Then, Samantha and Mamma Lottie finished eating and left the buffet. Mamma Lottie spoke out as she may have been a senior, but she *'knew a good man when she saw one.'*

"Ya'll jus' pass up all the good ones," said Mamma Lottie as Samantha just thought words of her own to herself and smiled.

Soon, about the sixth time or so, the bartender introduced himself.

"Hello, I've been seeing you pretty ladies for a while now. My name is Michael Douglas," said the bartender.

"Hello, I'm Samantha and this is Mamma Lottie," replied Samantha. Samantha was not giving him any more information about herself in fear of not really knowing anything about this guy. Samantha thought she knew Russell and Martin well, but as it turned out, she really didn't, and she didn't want to ever make those kinds of mistakes again. Plus, she was really not interested in Mike, period.

"I've been watching you all come for a while and I was wondering if I could call you sometime, Ms. Samantha," said Michael.

"Well, I don't know. I really don't give out my phone number," said Samantha as she remembered the tricky trauma of Martin's little nuisance of that phone call ordeal. Samantha glanced at Mamma Lottie from her peripheral vision. Mamma Lottie appeared to be looking directly at Samantha in that *you-better-not-let-this-one-get-away* type of look. Samantha was sort of interested but cautious, to be exact.

"I'll tell you what? Here's my number. Please call me sometime," said the bartender.

"Okay," replied Samantha as she took the piece of paper he handed her with his phone number written on it.

A Week Later

It was now time for Samantha and Mamma Lottie to eat at the buffet at the Isle of Capri again. They walked in and took a seat. Michael saw them and walked toward their table.

"You didn't call me, Samantha," said Michael.

"Yeah, I didn't know if you would be busy or not," said Samantha.

"I'm never too busy for you," Michael said, and it did get Samantha to cautiously smile at him.

"Please call me. I'd love to talk to you," said Mike.

"Okay, I'll call you," said Samantha.

Two Days Later

About two days later, Samantha did indeed call Michael. She just wanted someone to talk to; nothing else was her reason. She surely neither wanted a relationship nor did she want to get married again. She realized that her calling in life at this point was to take care of Mamma Lottie and herself, and she felt great doing just that.

At first, Mike and Samantha talked on the telephone for just thirty minutes. Then, the next time they talked for one hour. Later, they talked every day for an hour or two for weeks.

Months Passed

Mike and Samantha had been talking on the telephone for several months and Samantha looked forward to their conversations. He made her laugh so much and his conversations seemed genuine and heartfelt. He finally asked her out on a date and she reluctantly agreed.

Mike and Samantha met at a restaurant and both were looking their best to impress. They made small conversations at first and then the laughter came for both. They ultimately had a fabulous time and more dates followed. Mike even bought her a bouquet of red 'roses' and their thorns where sloughed off. Yes, Samantha did do a background check on Mike and she asked questions from everyone she'd known if they'd known him and she talked to his friends about him as well. Nothing but good things were said about Mike, and this pleased Samantha because she was falling in love with him.

Mike and Samantha had become best friends as a matter of fact. They began to tell each other about their past problems and neither would judge the other. Samantha tested the waters at first about telling Mike of her past and Mike never looked indifferent toward her. Then, she just laid it out to him about why she'd been so skeptical about relationships and he understood her emotions and was very compassionate, apologetic, and understanding toward her.

A Year or so Later

Over a year had passed and Samantha and Mike decided to get married. Samantha wondered if Mike was a facade and if the real Mike would soon come out and would be terrible. From all appearances, she just didn't get that vibe about him. She hesitantly said yes about marriage but knew she really loved Mike more than any other. It really felt like true love and not an infatuation or an obligation as before. Mike loved her as well and Samantha could tell by the way he treated her.

Samantha worried if Mike wanted children and she didn't want to go through another miscarriage or a broken relationship. She worried to no end and she felt she had to have this conversation with Mike before getting married. Mike advised her to 'trust in the Lord' and He would give them a child. Samantha had failed so many times but that's how faith works, not of our timing but God's. She'd lost a lot of faith when she'd prayed for her other babies to live and yet, they died.

Dianna

'Ever since the beginning of time, people have often lost faith in God as a result of their life experiences. Abraham lost faith when after twenty-five years of waiting for the promised son. He and Sarah decided that he should have one for their maid servant. The maid servant did indeed produce a child for Abraham. Yet, after waiting many more years, he and Sarah did indeed have a son. Abraham realized he should have waited the twenty-five-year span and he'd made the wrong choice. I can see their thinking because Sarah was ninety years old and their choice did seem right, but it was wrong and not what God advised them.

Many people face things that seem callous or brutal while others have been challenged with instructions existing from a secular viewpoint that rebuffs God's way of living. Whatever the situation is, we have all been there, waiting and wondering when or what is the right choice.

It is through involvements like these individuals when we start inquiring or questioning whether the God of the Holy Scriptures really has the answers to life's complications. Many begin to doubt the God Almighty, for they are weakened and their fate begins to falter. Because of these doubts, many stop worshipping, serving, believing, and trusting God's plan. They even stop communicating with God and begin to communicate with the internet and other worldly sources. Soon, their faith starts to diminish and eventually dies.

It doesn't matter how small our faith is. God wants us to reach out to Him. When there is little reason to trust Him, God wants us to believe in Him. In the Book of Job, God shows how He used Job in times of much turmoil and difficulty. Job experienced deep grief from the loss of his children, huge monetary losses, and had been stricken with a gravely physical illness. At a time such as this, it seemed that Job would have apparently had many causes to doubt God and lose his faith. It even was encouraged by the one person of whom you'd think would give him encouragement, his wife. Instead, at this point, she advised him that he should curse God and die.

Yet, Job reprimanded her for her thoughtless statement. Although Job, too, many times debated God as to why those things were occurring to him. No matter what, Job always trusted and returned to God in hopefulness. Job's declaration of faith in God is relevant for all who find their faith fluctuating as a conclusion of life exposures. 'Though He (God) slays me, yet will I trust in Him.' (Job 13:15).[1]

Whether you are up or have feelings of being far away from God in times of discouragement, reach out to God regardless. Press on through the little faith you have to inform Him precisely about how you feel and then examine His Word for the answers for your life. Encircle yourself with fervent Christian individuals who will comfort you through your times of wavering. You will not only experience the benediction of walking in relationship with a passionate God through the fluctuating encouragements and discouragements of life, but you can also preempt a time when you will be sustained by Him and guided into eternal glory.'

The Third Marriage

Mike and Samantha had gotten married and were settled in. Samantha revealed that she could discuss everything about her life with Mike and he would not blame or criticize her like her other husbands. He would never bring it up in her face the failed marriages or failed births. What Samantha saw in Mike when they first started dating was the same Mike after several months of dating and years into their marriage.

Hope

Now Samantha was thirty-six years old and she felt her biological clock was about to run out. Fearful, Samantha wondered what would happen if she got pregnant. It was a thorn that really pierced her heart. The weight she'd gained during her depression was harmful to her health as well. So, she lost weight. She went from two-hundred-plus pounds down to one hundred and thirty pounds by having a gastric bypass. A gastric bypass is a type of bariatric, or weight loss, surgery. She even stopped taking her birth-control pills in hopes of getting pregnant.

Bible Study

On one cool Wednesday night, Mike and Samantha had gone to Bible study and a lady by the name of Sister Nettie approached them.

"I need to speak with you all after church, you and Brother Mike," said Sister Nettie.

"Okay," said Samantha and Mike.

After Bible study, Sister Nettie approached both Mike and Samantha.

"You and Brother Mike are fixing to bring forth, but you have to keep the faith," she said. What she meant was they were going to have a baby. Mike just looked at Samantha. She looked at Mike and they both just smiled at each other as though Mike wanted to say, '*See I told ya so.*' Samantha was in disbelief to the news that Sister Nettie was advising her of. Never before had Samantha heard it prior to the last births. *Bring forth* meant that a baby would be indeed born and not another miscarriage.

A few weeks had passed and Samantha wasn't pregnant. Samantha approached Sister Nettie with the information as to why she hadn't gotten pregnant.

"Be patient, baby, and be positive, for God works in mysterious ways," advised Sister Nettie.

One day, Samantha had gone shopping for dresses. When trying on a dress, she noticed that she couldn't really get into her dress size, which was a size ten. So, she tried on a size twelve. This angered her because she didn't want to gain any weight, especially after the bypass surgery. She could really tell in her breast size that the dresses didn't fit the way they used to, for the dress was too tight in the upper portion.

The Incident

It was again time for Bible study, one Wednesday night. Mike and Samantha were heading that way. Mike was driving and Samantha was in the passenger seat. They got into a slight disagreement as Samantha felt somewhat surprisingly overwhelmed. This hardly ever happened throughout their entire three to four years of marriage. Samantha just hauled off and slapped Mike for no apparent reason. Mike abruptly stopped the vehicle and then he pulled over onto the side of the street. He got out of the car and walked over to the passenger side of the vehicle. Samantha was afraid that Mike was going to choke her to death or worse. Samantha thought about Martin killing his girlfriend and feared it was her time to leave this Earth. He opened the door.

"Don't you ever do that again, Samantha. I won't hit you and you don't hit me, okay?" asked Mike.

"Okay, baby, I'm sorry. I'm so sorry," replied Samantha apologetically. Mike walked back to the driver's seat and began to drive again.

"You're pregnant," Mike blurted out.

"Oh no, baby. I don't think so. I would have had some other symptoms by now," said Samantha.

"Naw, you're pregnant, baby," he said while shaking his head.

After Bible study that night, Mike and Samantha stopped at the nearest drugstore to get a pregnancy test. They headed home wondering if this would be the night that they'd waited for so long, a positive pregnancy result. Samantha never really had gotten a pregnancy test in the past because she felt she knew her body well enough that if she was pregnant, she would have known.

Samantha had gone in private to the bathroom to take the test. Her heart was pounding ninety to nothing and she feared she was pregnant, but was okay if she wasn't because of the past miscarriages. She closed her eyes before the results were available. She waited and waited even longer than the test results had allowed. She opened her eyes and the test revealed 'PREGNANT.' Samantha was indeed pregnant according to the test results. She slowly went to the living room area where Mike was beginning to watch television. She gave the good news to Mike and he was elated and jumped for joy.

"See, I told you so. I told you so, baby," said Mike as he began to hug Samantha.

Yet, deep down, Samantha had little faith and was afraid that she would lose this baby too, because now she was older than before when she was pregnant, much older. So, she just put on a somewhat fake happiness just to please Mike or, better yet, share his happiness.

Being Pregnant for the Sixth Time

At this time, Samantha worked at a local manufacturing company. Her boss advised her that the dye at the company could get into her bloodstream and harm her baby. She really didn't want to take any chances, so she quit.

Samantha surrounded herself with good, godly people. She also surrounded herself with people of rich faith, since she had lacked so much because of past experiences. She sought out good people and talked about God's goodness with everyone she came in contact with.

Striving to grow spiritually in faith would be difficult at first for Samantha. She felt that she didn't belong around faithful people because she was not as spiritually fit as her new friends or as Mike. As she matured in her walk with Jesus, it became much easier. She and Mike often talked about God and trusting in Him when Samantha had shown little faith. As they had accepted each other as husband and wife, they entrusted their spiritual growth to God to work His spirit within them. As they daily sought the Lord, they began to create an atmosphere of encouragement between themselves and their new friends.

One day, while Mike and Samantha were lying in bed getting ready for the next morning, they talked about this birth.

"Mike," said Samantha.

"Yeah, baby," replied Mike.

"What if… what if I have another miscarriage?" asked Samantha.

"God promised us a baby, not a miscarriage, Samantha, and that's what I've been praying to God about, a newborn baby," said Mike. Samantha was quiet after Mike's response, quiet of inward thoughts of previous prayers and previous faith.

"I love you, Mike," said Samantha.

"I love you too, baby," replied Mike.

Chapter 18
Fearful Samantha

Samantha Was Afraid

Wondering if there was anything to improve the chances of carrying the baby to full term after having five miscarriages, Samantha's doctor advised her that one in four pregnancies ends this way. Yet, Samantha felt through the grace of God that she could have a healthy child and hoped that she would be on the positive side of the statistics for once. She was slightly fearful that this one would end just as the others, and Mike, the one she truly loved from the bottom of her heart, would be so hurt. Samantha said a silent prayer:

"Dear Lord, help me to give this longing to you. Help me to surrender all my cares upon your care. I have laid down so many other dreams in the past years, but maybe this one is my deepest desire. I really, really want a child, so help me to trust you more and more as I wait on you and your unchanging hands."

Having the miscarriages were terrible experiences for Samantha. Twenty weeks' pregnancy in all her previous pregnancies was very agonizing and excruciating. Yet, all her hopes, excitement, and fears would be dashed in faith for the new life that was growing inside of her. Having mixed emotions, she'd often question herself as she wondered if getting pregnant was even a good idea in the first place. She didn't want another loss and the endeavor was so scary. She was even afraid of being happy, which may seem selfish, but how else was she to feel?

Thinking negatively was unhelpful for Samantha. Yet, not all people react with the same amount of grief and emotions after a miscarriage, or react the way she had if they'd gotten pregnant again. However, many people do.

There was a rational part of Samantha's brain that knew that believing in and getting excited about this pregnancy would now somehow be gone. Whether she knew it or not, she probably would always be scarred emotionally by the loss of her babies.

Being pregnant again after a miscarriage, an individual can feel an assortment of emotional expressions, including anxiety, distracting thoughts, and even post-traumatic stress disorder (PTSD) or anxiety attacks. Sometimes, Samantha's emotions would come in waves. Other times, they may peak around the time of her previous losses. They may spike every time she had an appointment at the doctor's office or looking at a couple riding a motorcycle.

Dianna

'Everyone deals with a miscarriage in dissimilar ways. Some individuals may choose to grieve the demise. On the other hand, another may even celebrate it in some fashion. Many individuals may discover it useful to depend on and open up their emotions to an entrusted loved one or possibly someone who has gone through the ordeal themselves. There are individuals who may take comfort from counseling, group therapy, or some type of professional therapy service.'

With new and updated technology, Samantha did have a better chance of carrying this child to full term. However, Samantha was fearful within, as she had been through letdowns so many times before. As she confided in her doctor, he explained that there were many reasons a woman could have miscarriage other than cervical insufficiency.

Dianna

'It has been studied that there are many causes of miscarriages. They are not limited to any one particular problem. A few problems may have been attributed to encompass thyroid dysfunction, whether too high or too low, progesterone levels, unmanageable diabetes that had never been diagnosed, intrauterine lesions or scarring from previous surgeries or diseases, uterine irregularities due to large uterine fibroids, infections, autoimmune diseases

such as lupus, and subjection to unquestioned chemicals. Factors such as these should be examined by a physician going forward.'

Being afraid had engulfed Samantha's life. She trusted God, but she feared the same would occur as before. She remembered being excited at first only to being letdown in the end. She found herself going to use the toilet at night. After using it she would turn on the light just to see and scrutinize the toilet paper, looking for signs of bleeding, as this was a sign a miscarriage was on the way. She looked for a pinprick thorn of blood each and every day which enhanced her PTSD. She tried not to let the fearfulness overtake her mind to the point of agitating another miscarriage, but she just couldn't help it.

Samantha continually read the Bible daily. She was supported by Mike and her other friends that this baby would be born. Faith was what you call it and Mike and Samantha had increased in a lot of it.

Due to Samantha's sorrows, she tried to seek out the sweetness and the good that was not often associated with the experience of miscarriage. It was something that only those who'd been there would understand. She sought out those memorable moments that were frequently hidden by the pain and agony. She found peace in extending herself to others, using her experiences to provide hope and comfort. Samantha could always remember with great solemnity and gratitude of Him, Jesus Christ, who suffered the most to make it all right for her. By doing this, she could be strengthened to bear her burdens in peace, and then, the works of God might be manifested.

Approaching Twenty Weeks

Samantha was now sixteen weeks' pregnant. She was fast approaching twenty weeks, the same twenty weeks where she'd lost her other five children. Reminding God as to what He'd said in His Word, Samantha read Psalm forty, daily.

1. *I waited patiently for the Lord;*
2. *He turned to me and heard my cry.*
3. *He lifted me out of my slimy pit, out of the mud and mire; He set my foot on a rock and gave me a firm place to stand.*
4. *He put a new song in my mouth, a hymn of praise to our God.*

5. *Many will see and fear the Lord and put their trust in Him.*
6. *Blessed is the one who trusts in the Lord who does not look to the proud, to those who turn aside to false gods.*
7. *Many, Lord, my God, are the wonders you have done, the things you planned for us.*
8. *None can compare with you; were I to speak and tell of your deeds, they would be too many to declare.* [2]

Over next few weeks, Samantha had become strong in her faith. Now refusing to believe that she'd lose this one was out of the question for Samantha as well as Mike. They believed and did not doubt the Lord. Faith works with prayer, and they both prayed fervently. Samantha really, really wanted a baby with Mike. Many times, Mike and Samantha would get on their knees and pray together. One day, they did just that as Mike began to pray.

Mike

"Dear Lord, in your Word, David said some trust in chariots or horses. I trust in the name of the Lord, my God. [2] We choose to walk in strength of our Savior. We choose to rest in our Redeemer and we choose to endure because of Emmanuel-God with us. God Before us and beside us. Walk with us, dear Lord, talk with us dear Lord, and please save our baby, dear Lord. In Jesus' name, Amen."

Trouble in Paradise

It was now twenty weeks that Samantha had been pregnant, and she started to hemorrhage in her abdomen. She was rushed to the emergency room and the closest one would be at the charity hospital. Dr. Bryce was his name, and he was one of the doctors that would be taking care of her. He got a little background of her past miscarriages as he read her chart. Samantha updated him about her past and even more about her past sexual assaults. He was heartfelt.

"We're gonna do all we can, Mrs. Douglas, but ultimately it's up to God," said Dr. Bryce. *'Wow,'* Samantha said to herself. At least this doctor believed, had the faith in God, and had knowledge to help save this baby's life and he'd spoken it aloud.

Later, another doctor entered Samantha's room, a student doctor. After administering several tests, he advised her that her sugar level was at borderline.

"Your sugar level is at borderline. Did you know that?" asked the student doctor.

"No, I didn't," said Samantha.

"Can you read?" the student doctor asked her in a sarcastic way.

"Yes, and I have insurance and I don't have to be here," Samantha replied.

"Well, a lot of ya'll can't read," said the student doctor. Samantha refused to let this student doctor make her angry and cause another miscarriage. She couldn't help but think that if this student doctor really talked down to the patients that hadn't any insurance, how would he help her with this fragile baby? This really wasn't worth the time of day for Samantha to argue with this student doctor, for she wanted to pass the test that God had set before her. The test of love should be shown during times of confrontations. That was 'what Jesus would do.'

A Thorny Miscarriage Is Threatened

Another doctor by the name of Dr. St. John examined Samantha later that same day and he decided to stitch up Samantha's womb a little tighter to stop the baby from coming out, for Samantha was starting to dilate. Samantha was in a lot of pain and all of a sudden, she looked down at the bottom half of her body. She was beginning to feel the baby exiting her womb.

"The baby's coming out! The baby's coming out!" screamed Samantha.

"Get her to surgery, STAT. This woman could die!" yelled Dr. Bryce.

Once Samantha had gotten to surgery, other doctors were just standing around and not giving her anything for the excruciating pain she suffered. The baby was ready to come out prematurely. But in that day and time, new technology and a deep faith in God were on her side.

Faith, Hope and Love

After being in such excruciating pain, the doctors finally gave Samantha pain medication, and this relaxed her. After a while, the baby was born by breech-birth. It was a boy. He was due to be born on November 22, but instead he was born September 3. He weighed three pounds and one oz.

Samantha vaguely saw the baby being born and was fearful because she was not out of the woods yet. The baby wasn't crying as most babies do when being delivered. The baby was being well examined by doctors and nurses.

After a while, one doctor advised Samantha and Mike that the baby would be blind for the rest of his life. Another doctor advised them that the baby would not be able to breathe on its own due to the delivery complications.

"There would be other complications that accompany this baby," explained the doctors to the couple.

Yet, Mike prayed because Samantha, by now, was out of it due to the heavy medications the doctors had given her.

Mike

"Dear Lord, sometimes I think I fear that which I don't understand. I see people with certain disabilities, and they say my baby may have some and I'm not sure how to react. Please help us to be loving and kind, treating our baby with love and nourishment no matter what. Heal his little body to grow and become strong. You love all of us regardless of age, race, or if we have a disability or not. We all are made in your image, so please, look down on our child and make him brand-new. In Jesus' name, Amen."

The Doctors' Diagnosis

After the doctors had worked on the baby for a long period of time, Samantha was dosing in and out from the pain medication. Soon, Samantha would feel better to get in a wheelchair to see the baby through a glass window. Mike and Samantha weren't able to hold the baby because he was being attended by doctors and hospital staff in ICU. They could, however, see the baby through this glass window as he was hooked up to monitors. They ultimately named the baby Joshua.

The doctors later revealed to them, while in the hospital room, that the baby would neither be blind nor have to use a breathing machine for the rest of his life. Mike fell to his knees and praised God openly.

"Thank you, Lord, for your grace, blessings, and answering our prayers."

Samantha and Mike

Giving birth to their first child was a miracle. The third of September was the most exciting day of Samantha and Mike's life. Samantha's been waiting for this day for the past fifteen years. Finally, Samantha was going to take her child home one day from the hospital, being a mother instead of walking away from the hospital in sadness and gloom. Smiles and flowers were what Samantha received from friends and Mike as well, roses to be more exact.

Loads of 'thank you, Lord' came out of the mouths of the parents, pastors, family, and friends. The doctors were elated that they'd played a part in making this family's dreams come true. They'd found out that Samantha had had five miscarriages in the past and many tears were shed from the staff. These were good days for the hospital and the couple was blessed.

Home with Joshua

Now it was time to go home and prepare being a parent. Once home, the couple settled into their new family lifestyle. It was time for Mike to rush out and get a crib, clothing, and other baby needs. Even though Samantha and Mike trusted in the Lord to allow this baby to be born, Samantha just couldn't bring herself to buy clothing or baby needs until the baby was actually born.

Mike had asked Samantha on a couple of occasions as to why she wasn't buying baby clothes or baby furniture. She just really didn't want to talk about this particular subject. After a while, he'd figured it out on his own. So many times when Samantha had bought cute little clothing, colorful baby furniture, and angelic baby paintings for the wall for her other babies, she would only be left in despair. When losing them, she'd have to come home to their reminder of what wasn't going to be, a brand-new life in the home.

Samantha would have to give the baby things away to friends or to the Salvation Army, while other times she would just smash and trash everything in a fit of anger. Every time Mike would ask her, she would shy away from the conversation. Even though Mike had never experienced the feeling of coming home to empty baby reminders, he understood and didn't pressure her, for he knew deep down in his heart what she was going through. I guess you could say she *still had the faith, but just-in-case* attitude.

The Brand-New Baby

Who needs an alarm clock when a baby wakes up at the crack of dawn, and Joshua was no exception. Formula and diapers were a must because selfishness went away a long time ago. That was okay; Joshua was well worth it.

In the first couple of weeks when the baby was released from the hospital, Samantha and Mike experienced the painful and joyful process of rearranging their expectations and placed them in line with the actual reality of a tiny infant, rather than nice and pretty fantasies. With a baby, none of it lasts, good, bad, or indifference. It was the incredible poignancy of a having a child.

After days of loving on his baby and wife, Mike headed back to work. Going to work to care for his family was what Mike really loved about life. He had a pep in his stride and always told jokes to his co-workers because he was so happy that the Lord had blessed him and his wife with a son.

Mike's prayers were now fulfilled, and giving God thanksgiving, honor, and praise was what he did hourly. He'd pray at work and at home for this gift of life. He was a changed man and he showed it to whoever came his way.

Mike

"Lord, Thank you for this treasured blessing! There seems to be no greater physical gift than this sweet bundle of joy sent straight from you. His perfect little fingers and toes, the way he smells like heaven, the love that bubbles up is unmatched in its depth. It's a wonderful kind of overwhelming love.

Please bless our baby, Lord. Place a shield of protection around his little body and guard him as he grows. Keep him safe and healthy, Lord. Help this dear one to know he is deeply, wholly, and forever loved – first by you and then by so many of us. Bless this baby, Lord, and bless my wife and me. Help us to adjust to our new normal as we welcome a whole new person into our lives, hearts, and home. Give us even one whole night of sleep, and give us strength and energy when the nights are short. Blanket our home in peace, grace, and love.

Thank You, Lord, for this new life. We praise and thank you for your good and perfect creation. In Jesus' name. Amen."

Chapter 19
The Baby

Joshua Is Three Months Old

For the first three months of parenthood, Samantha and Mike were the most excited parents in the world, however drained. They were suddenly in charge of the total care of this tiny little bundle of joy. Joshua didn't cry a lot but was awakened at odd times of the night and mornings. Mike and Samantha had taken turns to care for him and sometimes they would awaken together.

Joshua's early weeks were chaotic. However, as important as it was to see the baby's needs, it was equally important that their own needs were being met. After all, a healthy and happy parent meant that the baby would be happy and healthy.

Samantha

For Samantha, taking care of herself was vital. For new mothers, Samantha has some advice for women who have lost a child previously, and now have a brand new life to care for:

'Self-care is very important if you're going to get through the first three months of caring for your newborn. One must realize that your long-awaited bundle of joy will be so much better off being raised by a mother who tends to her cognitive, psychological, and physical wellbeing. If you need to pay for a little extra help, then do so and don't be too proud to ask.

Moreover, while new mothers shouldn't sense the need to pursue the misconception of getting their pre-baby figure back, it is imperative to encompass body-conditioning or exercise into your regimen. Exercise not only supports your physical health and postpartum recuperation but it's also important for administering tension and your cognitive wellbeing.'

Joshua Was Now Eight Months Old

Now Joshua was eight months old and the apple of his parents' eye, especially Samantha's. Breastfeeding him was perfectly fine. That was until the baby began to have stomach problems. Of course, Samantha had taken Josh to the pediatrician. The pediatrician advised Samantha to stop breastfeeding and start administering milk formula so that he could gain weight because he seemed to be underweight for his age.

This particular formula that the doctor advised had given little Joshua a rash, it seemed. Of course, Samantha had taken him back to the doctor. The doctor had given the baby many tests but could not figure out why Joshua was having a tiny rash. The rash had become much worse over the course of a couple of weeks.

What was so agonizing about the rash was that Josh was too little to scratch, as he only cried instead. Samantha advises that a newborn's skin is susceptible to breakouts and rashes of all varieties and most of these are harmless and go away on their own. Samantha has learned a great deal about different types of rashes and wants to pass them along to you.

Ordinary Rashes in Newborns

***Rose pimples** many times are thought to be originated by some type of subjection in the womb due to hormones from the mother. Relax. Only time is needed to heal, and not treatments. This can last a short time up to weeks on your child's skin.*

***Erythema toxicum** is another ordinary rash the newborns have. Its cause is unknown. This rash has red patches with ill-defined circumferences that are slightly raised. It may have a tiny yellow or white dot in the middle and it disappears, without treatment, after a few days. It can take a few weeks to go.*

***Parched, shedding skin** is a rash that can be seen in virtually all healthy babies but is primarily obvious in babies born a few days or weeks late. The fundamental skin is completely remarkable, moist, and soft.*

Tiny white bumps on the face and nose can result from obstructed oil glands. The bumps will disappear when the baby's oil glands open up after a few days or weeks.

Salmon patches, better known as the 'stork bit,' appear at the neck of the baby. An 'angel kiss' between their eyes is just simple nests of blood vessels. It is probably due to the mother's hormones that soon fade away on their own after a few weeks.

Jaundice is the yellowing on the child's eyes and skin. It is a breakdown of excess red blood cells. If the bilirubin levels are very elevated, little white or blue light may be placed on the baby's skin by your physician to lower the levels.

Mongolian spots are very ordinary rashes on any location of the baby's skin. Dark-skinned babies are especially prone to it. It is bluish-gray in color, similar to a bruise, and is flat. It can be tiny or huge. Some type of pigment in the skin is the cause that doesn't reach the top layer as the child's skin was being formed. Relax. They are harmless and fade away in time.

New rashes may be visible in babies after a few days, weeks, or even months. Sometimes, a baby's rash would accompany fever, lethargy, or a cough. It would be revealed about the type of rash Josh had, and of course, it was a thorn. Neither Samantha nor I, are physicians. Any rash should be checked out by a medical doctor.

Chapter 20
The Close Relative

Enquiring Minds

Ever wanted to know what happened to Samantha's close relative? He's still living to this day, as of 2021. He's very instrumental in the church and has a high position there. Samantha feels in her heart that he has never changed his ways of molesting and raping little girls and he could still be an *undocumented pedophile.*

Samantha remembered one day when she was about eleven or twelve years old. He had come over to their residence just for another visit. Samantha happened down the stairs as her close relative didn't see her. She suddenly walked into the presence of her close relative and one of her very younger nieces who was four years old at the time. Simultaneously, the niece had come into the same room with the close relative, a grown man.

"There goes my girlfriend," the close relative said to the niece. Samantha wondered if he was molesting her niece the very same way he'd molested her.

This same relative had gotten married before and his wife eventually died. He had always been in and out of relationships, mostly with women who'd already had children. This seemed to be his ultimate M.O.

The close male relative has *never* apologized for the molestations and sexual assaults to this day. The two keep their distances whenever and wherever they'd accidentally meet up, but he really avoided her at all cost. Samantha's presence made him feel uncomfortable so he just avoided her.

I, Dianna Thomas, was curious about the relationship between Samantha and her rapist today.

Samantha

"*Whenever we would have a gathering of some kind at a relative's house, if I came outside in the backyard and if he was outside, he would leave to go inside. If he was inside and if I came inside where he was at, he would leave to go outside. He could never be in the same room with me. We only spoke to each other and never had a conversation between the two of us. When he did speak, he'd always look down, for he could never look me in the eye. We were never in the room at the same time for any length of time. We had never had a conversation with each other, ever, because if I was there, he was not going to stay long and I didn't care what the occasion would be. It could have been Christmas at a relative's house and the entire family would be close by. My close relative would just leave sometimes if I was there.*

On one sunny day, I was taking out my trash to the curb. Before I got to the curb, my close relative just so happened to drive by. He got out of his vehicle and took the trashcan away from me and placed it on the curb himself. We never spoke a word. How awkward it was for my relative and me! It was as if he wanted to say something to me, but just didn't have the courage to do so. I didn't open my mouth and neither did he. He had every opportunity to say, 'I'm sorry for what I'd done to you as a child back then,' but he never opened his mouth.

He left me alone after I'd stabbed him. Surely, he wasn't expecting for me to apologize, because I never did. Surely, he knew he'd had it coming. I was a child and he was a grown man. He did have a drug and alcohol problem, but that was no excuse. He could have become an addict because of the guilt of taking away a child's innocence, not because he'd excused himself but because he was an addict.

My friend that he'd molested and raped as well now has a good relationship with him as though nothing had ever happened. They laugh and talk on several occasions. They go out on double dates as well as out to eat. She even cooks for him. I probably will never reach that point in my life because of the hurt and disrespect he'd shown me. I don't hate him because that's ungodly, and Jesus wants us to forgive and pray for those that hurt us and who've wronged us. I have somewhat forgiven him but not to the point of communication, let alone cook for him, if you know what I mean. I'm just not there yet.

There would be times I'd hate him and blamed him for the many miscarriages I'd had. Being torn as a little girl, I have no doubt the rapes were the reason for my weak and torn body. He'd caused five little babies to die. He was a murderer. I hated him. Yet, on the other hand I don't hate him, for then he would win again by taking over my mind and not allowing me to move forward and live a fulfilling life. If I'd carried that hate into a new beginning of my life, it would have been destructive. I wanted to live a life of love, harmony, respect, and joy. It's a funny thing trying to be obedient to Jesus."

Samantha shared with me that one day, she found out that her close relative was going to get married. That was okay in and of itself, for what did Samantha care about his life? Then, she found out that the lady he was going to marry had a young daughter. That changed everything for Samantha.

One day, Samantha decided to inform the lady to rethink about marrying this close relative because of what he'd done to her as a child. Samantha told the lady of her experiences and how he'd hurt her while growing up. This lady was very educated and worked for the local school system. To Samantha's surprise, the lady advised her that she felt that this close relative was a changed man and the lady married him *anyway*.

Later, Samantha found out her close male relative had made his wife's daughter, who was a very young teenager, dress up as though she was a little girl, since she was past the four-year-old stage. That was when she knew that he was up to his no-good tricks again.

Yet, suddenly, his wife died after having some type of local surgery. His wife left everything, such as her personal belongings and insurance policies, to her daughter and nothing for her close relative. She must have found out that Samantha's warnings were true and he'd maybe done the same things to the young teenager as he had done to her. Samantha has no proof of this, of course, but she has had strong feelings about it, because a leopard can't change its spots, ever. The signs were there though.

Can Pedophiles Change?

It was very hard for me, the author, to wrap my mind around how a grown person can be interested in a child sexually. Are they monsters, sick, or sick monsters? Amazingly, studies have shed light on some causes and effects of a pedophile.

Causes/Effects

"The ultimate result and final conclusions of pedophilia, and other paraphilias, are not confirmed. There is some verification that pedophilia may be inherited, though it is not clear as to whether its origins are <u>genetic</u> or learned conduct.

Another prospective element in the establishment of 'pedophilias' is the history of <u>prepubescent</u> sexual abuse. However, this has not been manifested. Behavioral competency representations recommend that a youth, who is the recipient or spectator of unsuitable sexual behaviors, may become accustomed to emulating these identical behaviors. When older, these individuals, denied of ordinary societal and sexual exposure, may search appeasement through reduced socially reasonable methods.

Physiological prototypes are analyzing the prospective correlation amidst <u>hormones</u> and behavior, specifically the role of <u>hostility</u> and male sexual hormones. Research has studied and revealed that pedophiles may be short in stature. They are more than likely to be left-handed. They may even have a lower IQ than mainstream society. Cerebrum scans declare that their white matter is less. That's the connective circuitry in the cerebrum. Thus, they are more than likely been afflicted by some childhood head injury than non-pedophiles, according to a study.

Many pedophiles may have become mindful of their sexual curiosity in children around the time of pubescence. Research has discovered that pedophilia may be a permanent ailment, but pedophilic affliction comprises components that can alter over time. Their behaviors can encompass deprivation, diminish of psychosocial skills, and have the propensity to act on cravings."

Treatment

"Moreover, research has also disproven the consciousness that sex offenders are substantially susceptible to recidivism. In actuality, rates are lower for recidivism in sex offenses than for all other major types of crimes. Additional research has found that only approximately three percent of child

molesters execute another sex crime within three years of being discharged from a penal institution. Amazingly, meta-analysis of hundreds of studies corroborates that once they are recognized, most convicted offenders never sexually reoffend. One study advised that not all sex offenders who victimize children are pedophiles; only about forty percent of convicted sex offenders meet the diagnostic specification for the condition.

Although medical care may help pedophiles withstand acting on their magnetism to children, many do not obtain medical assistance in as much as the uncertainty of lawful repercussions because of licensed professionals have an obligatory reporting law, including psychotherapist, counselors, and medical experts. For individuals with pedophilic conditions who, on the other hand, do obtain support, research proposes that <u>cognitive</u> conduct in medical care representations may be beneficial. Considerable representations may incorporate a type of aversive environment such as conflict of cognitive distortions and constructing of identification with victims, for instance, presenting videos of aftermaths to victims. Others include <u>self-confident</u> training, social skills training, <u>time-governance</u>, construction, regress or relapse impediment, locating a precursor to the conduct, and learning how to distort precursors and observation systems. Members of the family may aid in watching the convalescents' conduct with an understanding that it would lead to permanent maintenance.

Research has shown that there are certain medications that may be used in concurrence with <u>psychotherapy</u> to administer to pedophilic disorder. Many are geared toward the lowering of the sex drive, such as an anti-androgen. Further research has shown that the intensity of the sex drive is not compatibly interconnected to the behavior of paraphiliacs and high levels of cultivating <u>testosterone</u> do not make a male susceptible to paraphilias.

Further study has shown that hormones such as medroxy-progesterone acetate and cyproterone acetate may lessen the level of propagating testosterone, potentially lowering sex drive and hostility. These particular hormones, normally used in placement with performance and mental medical care, may lessen the incidences of sexual delusions, erections, and instigations of sexual conduct, including <u>masturbation</u> and sexual relations. There are many antidepressants that have also been established to lesson sex drive but have not efficiently focused on sexual imaginations.

Rearranging mental deformations require rectifying a pedophile's ideas that the child desires to be incorporated in the venture. Empathy training includes assisting the culprit to undertake on the viewpoint of the victim, have empathy with the victim, and understand the trauma and damage they are imposing. Affirmative stipulation approaches focuses on social skills training and substitutes a more suitable type of conduct. Restoring, for instance, requires administering the patient an instantaneous response or feedback, which in the long run may help him change his conduct.

There are prevention clinics, especially in other countries, that use <u>cognitive behavioral</u> techniques to train patients how to manage their sexual urges. One in particular has treated more than five thousand individuals who are willingly and brazenly searching for resources. Because some countries don't have mandatory reporting, it makes it easier for the individual to brazenly come forward for testing. These clinics also recommend psycho-pharmaceutical interventions, encompassing when necessary, and testosterone-lessoning <u>medication</u> to diminish sexual yearnings. The project's preliminary solutions appear encouraging. Candidates have been shown to reveal advancements in their capabilities and lessening in their convictions that may reinforce sexual exposure with children. However, it was a small sample.

It is difficult to determine the prognosis for lessoning pedophilic impulses, as long-established sexual desires about children can be laborious to alter. A professional medical expert can undertake to lessen the magnitude of desirability and aid a convalescent into emerging managing tactics, but the person must be prepared to discern that an enigma prevail and be inclined to engage in medical care for it to have an opportunity to flourish. Whether it's chemical approaches, dynamic psychotherapy, behavioral approaches, or even surgical interventions, each delivers mixed results. The answer is that it would take a lifelong prolongation and maintenance for a pedophile to have a successful treatment, as it seems to be the most pragmatic, feasible, and realistic way, and that takes a lifelong commitment."

Chapter 21
The Pit

The Pit of Thorns

In the past, before Mike and Joshua, Samantha would be in a pit of thorns because of the sexual assaults and loss of childhood. When you're in a pit, you begin to lose vision, and when you can't see your way out, you begin to look within. Once that happens, you begin to get very self-absorbed and have feelings of despair, depression, and discouragement, thus leading to alcohol, drugs, self-destruction, or the destruction of someone else. Then, the person may start to throw a 'pity party' for themselves in hopes that things will get better.

Nevertheless, that's not what God created Samantha for. He created her to make her a rock and to stand firm. Samantha wanted to break free from her abuser, but she just didn't know how, and as a child she was too vulnerable. God knew how she'd gotten in the pit and He showed her how to get out. She had to get out of the pit and stay out, only to return to share with those who were in that same pit or worse, a black thorny hole.

Sometimes, Samantha pretended to have it all together even as a Christian. It seemed that way from the outside, but within, she would sometimes be a total mess, a dark pit of a mess. After so many incidents of being sexually abused, failing marriages, and longing for a baby only to bury five, she was left in that solemn and dark pit.

How did she get out? First, she admitted to God that she was in a pit. King David, in Psalm 40:1-3, admitted that at times he was in a dark pit:

1. *I waited patiently for the Lord, and He inclined unto me, and heard my cry.*

2. *He brought me up also, out of the horrible pit, out of the miry clay, and set my feet upon a rock, and established many goings.*
3. *He had put a new song in my mouth, even praise unto our God. many shall see it, and fear, and shall trust in the Lord. 2*

Whether we want to admit it or not, the majority of people are living in a pit or with depression. Tragedy after tragedy, failure after failure, shattered hopes, and wrecked dreams will get you there, sometimes of your own doing while other times it's because of what someone has done to you. Getting the help from a *trusting hand* to lift you out of this hole is the answer. It's very difficult to do it alone.

If you're an alcoholic, have a gambling addition, a sex addiction, or have a drug addiction, you're in a pit. If you suffer from depression, or if you are very discouraged, you're in a pit. If you've been sexually assaulted, abused by your mate, or have lost loved ones that were so dear, you're in a pit. You can go to church or work all dressed up but be in a pit without even knowing it.

Dianna

'The fact that depression may transpire only once during your life, individuals ordinarily have numerous incidents. It is during these episodes that evidence usually occurs throughout the day, practically every day, and it may consist of:

- *Periods of melancholy or unhappiness, crying, hollowness, or emptiness or despairing or hopelessness*
- *Intervals of having angry explosions or outbursts, short-temperament, irritability, disappointments, or frustration*
- *Phases of loss of attentiveness or amusement in most or all conventional engagements, such as hobbies, sports, or sex*
- *Durations of sleep disruptions, including insomnia or oversleeping*
- *Episodes of exhaustion and lack of energy such that even minimal tasks take exceptional endeavor*
- *Intervals of loss of appetite, weight loss, or even intensified hunger for food and weight gain*

- *Periods of nervousness or anxiety, disquiet or agitation, or restlessness*
- *Phases of sluggish thinking, speaking, or body motions*
- *Intervals of feeling unproductive or worthlessness or self-reproach or guilt, fixating on past failures or self-blame*
- *Problems of reflecting, focusing, remembering things, and making decisions*
- *Repeated or sporadic pondering of death, suicidal thoughts, suicide attempts, or suicide itself*
- *Unexplained body ailments, such as headaches or back pain*

For many individuals with depression, signs generally are serious enough to cause apparent complications in their day-to-day activities, such as social activities, relationships with others, work, or school. It usually starts gradual and builds up to seriousness. Many individuals may feel predominantly disconsolate, gloomy, dejected, downcast, miserable, or unhappy without really knowing why.'

A Bible Story

There are several stories in the Bible, of characters who were actually in a pit or a dark place. It tells of how they'd overcome such deep despair and turmoil. Many Bible characters did so by obeying the Lord, which seemed hard at first because the devil had so many bad choices he wanted them to use so that they could fall and stay in that pit.

A good Bible story is the story of Joseph in the book of Genesis. Joseph was his dad's favorite of his other brothers. Joseph, the youngest of twelve brothers, had a dream and he told his brothers of the dream. He said, "I dreamed that you would bow down to me." This infuriated his brothers to no end.

Dianna

'Soon, Joseph told these two dreams to his brothers. They deplored him for the insinuations that the family would be yielding and bowing down to Joseph. The brothers had become enraged with jealousy. Even though Joseph was his father's favorite son because he'd had him in his old age, he too

would ponder over the words Joseph had been telling the family about these dreams. This is in Genesis 37:1-11. Then, the brothers saw an opportunity as they were in the field, feeding the flocks. From afar, they saw Joseph and they began to come up with a plot to kill him.

Once Joseph had gotten closer, the brothers turned to him suddenly and confiscated him of the very colorful coat their father had made exclusively for Joseph. Afterwards, they contemplated as to what would be their next move. At the request of their brother Rueben, instead of secretly killing him as the brothers wanted, they decided to just throw him in a pit in the wilderness so that bloodshed would not be on their hands.

So, they threw him in a pit. Soon, the brothers instantaneously saw a camel caravan of Ishmaelites from Gilead walk by. The Ishmaelites were carrying perfumes, spices, and myrrh to Egypt for trade. Of the twelve brothers, Judah was the strongest. He was hesitant about the plot of killing their brother Joseph and he suggested that he be sold to the Ishmaelites into slavery. The Ishmaelites paid twenty pieces of silver for Joseph.

The plot wasn't fully completed because now the brothers had to explain to their father, Jacob, as to what had happened to his favorite son, Joseph. The plot thickened. The brothers grabbed Joseph's colorful coat, they killed a goat, and spilled its blood all over the coat and ran back to their father Jacob and they lied to him, explaining that their beloved Joseph had been captured and killed by wild animals.

Potiphar's House

It was clear in the Biblical story of Joseph who finally got out of the dark pit, at the request of Judah and was sold into a miserable world of slavery by his brothers: "Come, let us sell him to the Ishmaelites," Genesis 37:27.[1] I assume that Joseph wondered along the way as to what he could have done to receive such treatment.

While in Egypt, the book of Genesis explains that a captain of the guards by the name of Potiphar 'bought Joseph from the Ishmaelites who had brought him down there.' Genesis 39:1[1]

Now Joseph was sold again and was serving in Potiphar's household quarters. During that time, Joseph had begun to flourish in everything he did because the God Yahweh was with him. Joseph had become Potiphar's personal servant because he'd found benevolence in his sight.

Then, Joseph became a superintendent and was promoted to oversee Potiphar's entire household. As time passed, Joseph had a secret admirer. This was no ordinary admirer like a slave girl. No, it was Potiphar's wife. His wife began to lust for Joseph as she'd sought to have an affair with him. Notwithstanding her persistence, he declined to have sex with her. Joseph had great terror and feared sinning against God. He also didn't want to be treacherous against the one who'd given him such favor, Potiphar.

Potiphar's wife, in days ahead, had become desperate for Joseph and begged for him to have sex with her. She caught him alone, one day, and got very seductively close to him. He tried to escape from her claws and when he did, she grabbed him by his cloak, leaving his garment torn from behind. Joseph ran fast and as far away from her as he could. Outraged by this act of running away, she took his garment and falsified claims to her husband that Joseph tried to have sex with her. This claim enraged Potiphar, and as a result, he threw Joseph in prison.

Joseph Sent to Prison

As time went on, during the time that Joseph was in prison, the warden placed him in charge of the other prisoners. Joseph probably said, "Here we go again." He was placed in a terrible situation that was not his fault, again. The warden must have seen something in Joseph that was trustworthy and decided to make him a leader of other inmates.

Shortly afterwards, Pharaoh's chief baker and chief cupbearer was thrown into prison because they had offended Pharaoh. Soon, they both had dreams and asked Joseph to help them to decipher them. Held in the hand of the chief cupbearer was a vine. This vine had three branches that had produced grapes. The cupbearer took them to Pharaoh and placed them in his cup.

On the head of the chief baker, however, were three baskets of bread. The bread was intended for pharaoh when some birds came by and ate the bread. Both chiefs took their dreams to Joseph to see what messages were intertwined in them.

Joseph told the cupbearer that he would be let out of prison and placed with the prominent job he'd had before being incarcerated. The chief baker had a different result from the meaning of his dream. Joseph told him that he was soon going to be hanged.

Furthermore, since Joseph had given the cupbearer this great news, Joseph only asked of him a favor once he had gotten in place. All Joseph wanted him to do was mention him to Pharaoh and allow him to be released from jail. Yet, once the cupbearer was in place, he forgot all about Joseph. The chief baker was indeed hanged and Joseph remained in jail for two more years.

Soon after two years had passed, Pharaoh had two dreams that troubled him. Pharaoh had dreamed of seven cows that were very lean. These lean cows had arisen out of the river and consumed another seven voluminous fat cows. The other dream that Pharaoh had was about seven withered ears of grain that gobbled seven fat ears.

Stay with me regarding this story. I'm going somewhere. Unable to decipher Pharaoh's dreams from his own wise men, that same cupbearer suddenly remembered the skillful interpreter Joseph. It was at this time that the cupbearer spoke of Joseph's expertise to Pharaoh.

Joseph was summoned to Pharaoh. Joseph did indeed interpret the dreams of Pharaoh by predicting that seven years of profound prosperity would be accompanied by seven years of profound famine. Joseph's infinite wisdom suggested that Pharaoh accumulated a surplus of grain during the years of plentifulness. He also advised him that when this famine ultimately came into effect, neighboring nations would 'roam and wander on the earth' and would have no choice but to come to Egypt and buy bread from him because Pharaoh's kingdom had smartly prepared for the seven-year drought. Pharaoh then took Joseph out of prison and placed Joseph in a very prominent position within the palace because he'd revealed the dreams correctly to him.

Brothers Sent to Egypt

The famine was indeed very severe. After years of nearly starving, Joseph's brothers had no choice but to go to Egypt at the request of their father Jacob/Israel to buy goods. Once in Egypt, they stood before this well-fed and well-dressed prominent leader, not knowing it was their brother Joseph. However, Joseph instantly recognized them from afar and treated them with kindness as he further disguised himself and spoke to them in Egyptian language using an interpreter. Joseph never used his native language, which was Hebrew, fearing they'd recognize him inevitably.

Joseph asked the brothers a series of questions. Once they'd responded, Joseph came up with the notion of accusing his brothers of being spies. The brothers pleaded for their lives and tried to convince him that their only purpose for being there was to buy grains for their family back in the land of Canaan. The brothers also told Joseph that they had left a younger brother Benjamin, Joseph's blood brother, back home. Joseph commanded that Benjamin be brought back to Egypt to demonstrate their trustworthiness.

The brothers were incarcerated for three days by Joseph. On that third day, Joseph had taken them out of prison to rehearse again that he wanted them to confirm their trustworthiness by going back home and bringing Benjamin back to Egypt with them when they returned. They were not to deviate from this plan and they understood.

The brothers consulted between themselves as they spoke in Hebrew, thinking that Joseph would not be able to understand them. The conversation between them came up about Joseph and the past as they'd remembered and reflected about the wrong they'd done to him back in the day, not knowing that the prominent leader was Joseph in the flesh. Joseph overheard and understood them conferring between themselves. Joseph had to remove himself from their presence because he was overwhelmed with emotion.

Joseph kindly sent the brothers back with nourishing food. However, he kept one brother, probably as ransom, as the remaining brothers went back to Canaan to their father. Once back in Canaan, the brothers told their father all that had materialized in Egypt. The brothers even noticed that when they had gotten out of jail and had returned home, all of their money sacks still had money in them and they were appalled.

The brothers told their father that this prominent leader had commanded them that they bring Benjamin back to Egypt before him to corroborate of their trustworthiness. Soon, when all of the grains had been consumed, their father advised his sons to return for more grains. With Judah and Reuben to help convince their father to allow Benjamin to join them for the terror of Egyptian retribution, their father relented.

While the brothers were headed back to Egypt along with Benjamin, they were in terror and were frightened because of the returned money in their money sacks. They didn't know what to think. Yet, once they returned to this prominent leader, as promised with Benjamin. The overwhelmed Joseph ultimately revealed to them that he was in fact their forgiving brother.

Eventually, their father who had grieved the loss of Joseph ever since he thought he'd died, went to Egypt and they all were prosperously reunited.'

Why This Story?

I chose this story because twice, Joseph was in a pit, a real pit, and didn't know where to turn. Years had passed and Joseph was still confined in Potiphar's prison, forgotten by the cupbearer even after Joseph had interpreted the dreams of Pharaoh. Was he forgotten by God? Was Samantha forgotten by God? In His own way and in His own time, God would provide. He did it for Joseph and he'll do it for you, me, and Samantha.

This episode in the life of Joseph brings us to a vantage point from which we may look backward and forward. Looking back, we must realize that Joseph's elevation was not the result of one lucky break but rather of a chain of painful but divinely purposed events. Had Joseph not been cruelly treated by his brothers and sold into slavery, he would never have been in Potiphar's house. Had Joseph not said 'no' to Potiphar's wife and been unjustly cast into prison with the cupbearer, he could never have been recommended to this prominent, affluential king.

What a beautiful illustration of Romans! 8:28:

"And we know that God causes all things to work together for good, to those who love God, to those who are called to His purpose."

Dianna

'Glancing from the beginning to the end of Joseph's story, we see that even though Joseph is the essential character of this section, he is not the exclusive recipient of God's attention and activity. Joseph was indeed blessed because of this. While there is a sense in which Joseph was blessed because of his faithfulness and trustworthiness, there is even an extensive interpretation that Joseph's advancement was not for his own prosperity as much as for his brothers' preservation. Joseph's position of prosperity and power empowered him to become the 'savior' of his brethren.

We must be humbled by the fact that while God cares for us as individuals, He often has an extensive motive for what He gives to us.

Ecclesiastical gifts, for instance, are not given for our own convenience so much as for the uplifting and building of others.'

Samantha wasn't picked on but picked out to be a blessing to someone. No, she didn't ask for it, neither did she deserve the harsh treatments, but God was using her to reach out and pick someone up out of their pit. That's why she wants this informative book written. Joseph was thrown into a dark pit the first time and the second into a prison of a pit not for something he'd done but for something someone had done to him.

If you've ever experienced a crisis in your life or persecution, if you've been mistreated by someone or got a raw deal, if life just keeps knocking you down or whatever your pit is, Samantha completely understands. She also understands that God understands. The story of Joseph is one that teaches us to be courageous in the midst of some of life's worst pits and prickly thorns.

Here are eight vital life lessons you can apply to your own life.

Dianna

1. *'A dream of Joseph was given by God. At the time, he couldn't understand why he had to suffer so much pain. Yet, way down, deep in his soul, he knew that Almighty God had a big vision for his life and in His time.*

2. *Thinking that God has forgotten about you and has turned His back on you is a tendency we all have when we've fallen into a pit. At this time, you should adhere especially harder to God. The Lord was with Joseph even when he was sold into slavery, and he ultimately prospered.*

3. *When we walk in long-term effects with God as Joseph did, and his testimony had become powerful, temptation will always come, but allow God's grace to cause you to escape and flee from sin and shield you from all of the enemy's deceptions.*

4. *Joseph always gave God the glory for his dreams and never took credit or misinterpreted them. He always knew they were a gift from God.*

5. *When we are honored with prosperity and success by God, we mustn't forget to first honor Him and honor others. In a time of*

desperate need of his family, it didn't stop Joseph from blessing the very ones that had sold him into slavery.

6. *Joseph learned to have humility throughout his journey. In order for God to lift Joseph up, He had to first lower him down so that he would be humble.*

7. *For those who've done you wrong, set your heart to forgive them. It keeps your heart from the deep-rooted destroyer of bitterness and resentment from the past and ultimately heals your relationships.*

8. *Gaining wealth is not true prosperity; it's in glorifying God by the way you live your life. He could have slept with Potiphar's wife deceptively, thinking he would have lived in prosperity afterwards. Joseph always tried to do what was right and continued to cultivate and strive for a relationship with God. This is authentic and true prosperity.'*

Jesus Christ

Of course, no one has suffered as much as our Lord and Savior Jesus Christ. He was an innocent man and he carried the weight of our sins on his back, a back that had been beaten so badly that layers upon layers of his skin were ripped off.

Dianna

'The sufferings of Jesus' life were more than just physical. He was exposed to a full range of human suffering to absolute proportion. The Holy Bible reveals that:

He was abandoned: *"Then all the disciples left him and fled." (Matthew 26:56).*

He was erroneously and falsely criticized by those in the crowd: *"Now the chief priests and the whole council were seeking false testimony against Jesus that they might put him to death, but they found none, though many false witnesses came forward." (Matthew 26:60)*

He was condemned and betrayed: *"Judas, would you betray the Son of Man with a kiss?" (Luke 22:48)*

He was taken captive and incarcerated: *"Then they came up and laid hands on Jesus and seized him." (Matthew 26:50)*

He was spat upon and severely beaten: *"Then they spat in his face and struck him. And some slapped him, saying, 'Prophesy to us, you Christ! Who is it that struck you?'"* *(Matthew 26:67-68)*

He was untruthfully denounced and accused by those in authority: *"But when he was accused by the chief priests and elders, he gave no answer."* *(Matthew 27:12)*

He was spurned and rejected: *"The governor again said to them, 'Which of the two do you want me to release for you?' And they said, 'Barabbas.' Pilate said to them, 'Then what shall I do with Jesus who is called Christ?' They all said, 'Let him be crucified.'"* *(Matthew 27:21-22)*

He was whipped and scourged: *"Then he released for them Barabbas, and having scourged Jesus, delivered him to be crucified."* *(Matthew 27:26)*

He was ridiculed and mocked: *"And kneeling before him, they mocked him, saying, 'Hail, King of the Jews!' And they spat on him and took the reed and struck him on the head."* *(Matthew 27:29-30)*

He was disdained: *"And those who passed by derided him, wagging their heads."* *(Matthew 27:39)*

He lost his life: *"And Jesus cried out again with a loud voice and yielded up his spirit."* *(Matthew 27:50)*

Jesus did all this voluntarily and willingly: *"And going a little farther, he fell on his face and prayed, saying, 'My Father, if it be possible, let this cup pass from me; nevertheless, not as I will, but as You will.'"* *(Matthew 26:39)*

He did this our deliverance: *"He himself bore our sins in his body on the tree, that we might die to sin and live to righteousness. By his wounds, you have been healed."* *(1 Peter 2:24)*

There were many more characters that suffered as well, but the story of Joseph, coupled with the story of Jesus, are two that many people can relate to, especially so for Samantha. Forgiveness was the key for Samantha to live the rest of her days in joy. Joseph had to forgive his brothers and Samantha had to forgive her close relative and ex-husbands. There were still troublesome days ahead for her, but God will always be there to get her out of the pit, the pit of thorns.

Chapter 22
A Thorn That Stings

Joshua

Now that Samantha and Mike had settled down into parenthood, little Joshua, their son, was about ten months old and was beginning to sleep longer at night. If you are a parent, then you know the routine. Very seldom does a newborn come into the world sleeping a complete eight hours throughout the night.

Every time the baby farted, it seemed that Samantha was taking him to the doctor to get checked out, literally. She was so cautious and overprotective of little Josh that the doctors had to slow her down and advise her that he would be okay and little things are not really a great concern. It was just a part of her being anxious and concerned that something may happen to Josh, Samantha felt.

The doctors did although advise her that little Josh wasn't gaining weight as he should have for his age. Samantha was breastfeeding him and she was on a vegetable and fruit diet to ensure a happy and healthy baby. The doctor advised her to stop breastfeeding and start giving him a high-calorie milk formula. Samantha did what the doctor ordered.

Soon, a little red spot, a rash, appeared on the back of Joshua's neck. A thorn was beginning to sprout. Again, Samantha took Josh to the doctor and after many tests, he couldn't figure out, at first, as to why the rash was occurring. When the tests finally came back, the doctors advised her that it was a skin disease called eczema – another thorn. He advised her to be careful of the soap she used and if the spot had gotten worse, he told her to bring him back to see him.

Eczema is a fairly common ailment that produces a rash to the skin. It makes a person's skin become itchy and extremely dry. This disease is especially prevalent in infants and young children but can continue into adulthood. Unfortunately, as of yet, there isn't a cure for eczema. However, there are treatments for when flare-ups occur.

Well, Joshua's eczema did get worse and a month later, it had spread from the top of his little head to the bottom of his little feet. The doctor advised Samantha and Mike that he'd never seen eczema that bad before on a person. As a matter of fact, it was the worse he'd ever seen in his career. He had given Samantha some steroids and skin cream and hoped it would clear up the eczema. It did clear him up for a while, but the eczema returned and had begun to spread again.

The doctor prescribed a medication called prednisone to Joshua. This medication was usually given to patients to treat conditions such as blood disorders, breathing problems, arthritis, severe skin diseases, cancer, eye problems, and immune system's disorders. Because Josh was so young, there would be side effects such as weakness, weight loss, nausea, muscle pains, headaches, tiredness, and dizziness. This too was a temporary fix and little Josh was always in agony because of the itching, discomfort, and the pain he'd suffer. Prednisone makes an individual rest well so that they would not scratch and possibly heal quicker. It would clear him up for a little while, but the eczema would always return, and as a matter of fact, it continued to only get worse.

Of course, this made Samantha and Mike get in agony as well just to see their little baby in such turmoil. Many doctors advised Samantha and Mike that they'd never seen eczema on a person that bad before. Mike and Samantha had heard about a holistic doctor, one that believed in natural healing, and thus, they started taking Josh to a holistic doctor named Dr. William.

Dianna

'Holistic medicine is a form of therapy that assesses the whole person – spirit, body, emotions, and mind – in the journey for optimal health and wellness. Their holistic medicine philosophy is that one can achieve optimal health by obtaining proper stability in life.

The whole person is made up of interdependent parts and if one part is not working correctly, all the other parts will be distressed. This is the practitioner's belief. In other words, it can cause a negative effect in their overall health imbalances such as their physical, emotional, or spiritual life.

Whether it's conventional medication or alternative therapies to treat a patient, a holistic doctor may use all forms of healthcare. For instance, if a person is suffering from a migraine headache and they visit a holistic doctor, instead of the patient leaving the office with loads of medications, the doctor will likely look at all potential factors that may be causing the headaches.' They may look at other health difficulties, sleeping habits, diet, stress, personal problems, or preferred spiritual practices. Their plans for treatments may incorporate medications to alleviate the symptoms or have lifestyle adjustments to help avert the recurring headaches.'

Dr. William started giving little Josh some herbs, frankincense oil, and lavender. He'd also given them black soap from Africa to bathe him in. Josh cleared up really, really well for a month, that is. Finally, it too stopped working and the severe eczema returned.

Mike and Samantha then had taken Josh to the Louisiana State Hospital, LSU, and the doctors noticed that Josh's lymph nodes were swollen, so they ran a battery of test on him because they feared it would be leukemia, a type of cancer. Samantha was distraught and had to lean on Mike for support to alleviate the feelings of grief and distress. Mike was crying and leaned on Samantha for comfort. They kept asking each other if each were okay. The doctor advised them to come back to get the results.

That night, Samantha and Mike went home to pray.

Samantha and Mike

"Dear Lord, our Heavenly Father, you have given us a spirit of love, power, and faith. We're not alone. Please go with us into battle. The battle is not our own. It belongs to you, my God. We refuse to fear or doubt. We call on the powerful name of God Almighty to see us through these troublesome days. Thank you for fighting for us, Lord. In Jesus's name. Amen."

Samantha

"After hearing the news that my baby may have cancer, my mind just went blank. I literally don't remember walking down the hallway or getting into the elevator to leave. I had to have left because I remembered being at home. My mind would not allow me to remember neither the hallway nor elevator.

I thought, 'Oh Lord, after all I'd been through, surely my baby doesn't have cancer.' When I finally got a baby after all these years, now he may have cancer. I just couldn't wrap my mind around it. Lord, you said you would not put more on us than we can bear, but Lord, I don't know about this trial."

Yet, when continually waiting for the test to return about whether Josh had cancer, days went by. Mike and Samantha were anxious. They prayed and prayed and prayed and prayed some more, many times together, other times apart. Many times, they prayed while driving to the grocery store and many times on bended knees.

Mike

"Lord, we feel like we're on a rollercoaster with our child's eczema. Some days, our emotions are stable and we feel good. Other days, we feel far from normal and just wish we could do all the daily tasks that others do so easily. Please steady our thoughts and feelings. Help us, oh Lord, to trust you to meet our needs, even with this disability with our son, day by day. Please, dear Lord, don't let him have cancer and heal his little body. In Jesus' name. Amen."

This trial really brought Mike and Samantha closer together. There would be times that they would just have to stop and hold each other and cry together. In other times, they would be somber in deep thought as the tears rolled down their faces.

The Doctor's Report

Now it was time to get the results back from LSU Hospital to see if Joshua had cancer. Samantha and Mike were in the doctor's office, holding hands as they had been all prayed up. Their anxiety hit a new level as they were waiting for the doctor to explain the test results. They'd tried to read his expression as he'd entered into the examining room. This doctor was emotionless though. He opened his mouth. It *wasn't* cancer, the doctor had revealed, and once he'd said that, you could literally see Mike and Samantha's chests lower at the same time in relief.

"Thank you, Lord Jesus, thank you!" Mike cried aloud. A moment passed as Mike tried to get his composure together; Samantha patted him on the back in comfort. Mike finally had gotten his equanimity back as the doctors at LSU explained that it was too *the worst case of eczema they'd ever seen*, something they'd heard all too often.

Several Months Later

By now, Josh had no skin on his little body, for he was pink all over because all of his skin had peeled off. His immune system was low because our skin protects our body and organs from all kinds of diseases. He was a sickly child and in a lot of pain as well.

Mike and Samantha had taken Joshua to another hospital, Schumpert Hospital. It was the same song and dance; *'It's the worst we have ever seen.'* They tried another hospital, Willis Knighton Hospital, and it was the same old song and dance; *'The worst case we've ever seen.'* Those were all the hospitals in Shreveport, and Mike and Samantha were mentally exhausted, and so was little Josh. At Willis Knighton, they advised the couple to take Josh to Arkansas Children's Hospital for a more advanced type of treatment.

Arkansas Children's Hospital

Mike and Samantha headed to Arkansas with Josh, and while there at the Arkansas Children's Hospital, Mike and Samantha learned that a lot of people from Africa had this type of eczema. They'd also learned that there was mild, moderate, and severe eczema. Of course, Josh had severe eczema. They also learned that not many people in the United States had severe eczema, only mild to moderate.

The doctors noticed the small patch of redness on Samantha's body and started to do some background on her family's history. It was revealed that many close relatives of Samantha had mild to moderate eczema, including her niece. They also revealed that on Mike's side of the family, there were close relatives that also had mild to moderate eczema. That meant that Josh had gotten a double whammy of eczema from both sides of his family.

After being in the Children's Hospital in Arkansas, the doctors again said *it was the worse they'd ever seen.* The doctors began to wrap little Josh up from head to toe to protect his body from diseases and hoped this method would help heal his skin back to its natural color, other than pink. Josh looked like a little mummy, his mom explained. It had made him feel so bad because he had the urge to scratch but couldn't because of the bandages. This was suffering to Josh as well as his parents.

Now What?

'Now what' was a good question because Mike had to return home to Shreveport in order to work to keep the bills paid. While there, Mike got desperately ill and had to be hospitalized. It was another thorn. Samantha was literally back and forth from the hospital in Shreveport with Mike and Arkansas with Josh.

Samantha didn't have a support system in place at the time and had no one to turn to for help. She was between hospitals and praying to get her family back to being normal again. Leaving Josh in the hospital to go and see Mike was one the hardest thing she had to do. Yet, it had to be done.

Mike

As it turned out, Mike had a big, big hole in his foot. He would put his sock over it and not let Samantha know because he didn't want her to worry about him or upset her, for she had so many tribulations in her life and because of Josh's health too. The hole in Mike's foot was due to a diabetic ulcer. Samantha said it was large enough to place her hand inside his foot. He almost had to have his leg amputated. Mike wasn't worried about himself; he was worried about his son, Josh. He placed his health last and it almost cost him a leg in the process.

From awards at work to employee-of-the-month awards to losing his job entirely was what Mike faced. Yes, Mike lost his job due to his health because he'd taken all of his vacation and sick time for Josh's health. Now, Samantha had to go to work. She'd worked two jobs just to make ends meet.

She did private sitting in the evenings and worked at a local hospital at daytime. On her days off and in the evening time, she was either at one hospital or another. She was worn thin, to say the least.

Samantha was born with strength. What she'd gone through in the past had made her a strong woman for her future. Trial after trial, tribulation after tribulation, thorn after thorn, Samantha, although weak, pressed on each day, one at a time. Many women couldn't endure what Samantha had had to withstand, but Samantha had an inner strength that kept her going in spite of the difficulties.

Finally, Josh was released from the Arkansas Hospital, but not without family-lifestyle changes. The doctors at the Arkansas Children's Hospital advised Samantha that she had to make changes around the house when she'd gotten home. Samantha had to be vigilant about the substances and materials that would lead to a breakout for Joshua. Some of the changes were white sheets and comforters only, no colored sheets. There were changes like different washing detergent, one that neither had dyes nor perfumes in them, changes like taking up all the carpet out of the house and just when they'd gotten a new tub, it had to be removed.

One evening, once Joshua returned home, he and Samantha were sitting on the couch. Josh, now age three, was sitting at one end and Samantha was on the other. Samantha began to feel overwhelmed, for she had had so much to deal with and was tired from working two jobs. She looked at little Josh all wrapped up in bandages and in pain. She started to cry.

"Why are you crying, Mommy?" asked Josh.

"Cause I can't do anything to help you, baby," cried Samantha. She further stated,

"I waited this long to have a baby and look what I have to go through," said Samantha. She was careful not to hurt his feelings or make him feel unwanted or unworthy.

"Mommy, you know why the enemy is attracted to my body?" asked Josh.

"Why, baby?" cried Samantha.

"Cause he can't have my soul," said Josh, at age three. Samantha, while being in amazement, just did boo-hoos all the more because he was taking it so well, considering the agony he'd been dealing with.

Josh was Samantha's strong-hold. His sickness had given her time to stop, look, and listen to every word Josh had to share. No matter how sick and troublesome Josh was, Samantha loved him dearly. Josh was exactly what Samantha wanted in a child.

One day, Samantha had learned from another mother, whose child was suffering from mild eczema, to change Josh's eating habits, such as taking fast foods out of his diet. That particular parent felt that it could have been what children were eating that triggered the eczema. Of course, there wouldn't be any fast foods in the Douglas household and it somewhat helped Joshua's illness, not much, but anything that would help him was fine with Samantha.

Chapter 23
Peace

Family

Soon, after a few months of torment, running errands, and getting in and out of doctors offices and hospitals, everything began to settle down in the Douglas household. Mike's foot started to heal and he went back to work at another job. Samantha let go one job and kept the other to be home with Josh. Mike had gotten a job of a security supervisor at a local facility. Josh's dressings still had to be changed to protect his skin. Samantha would always play gospel music every night so that Josh could calm down and stop scratching.

Daycare

Soon, Josh had healed enough and was old enough to go to daycare. He was so excited to be able to play with other children instead of being inside all the time. His entire spirits were lifted and so were Mike's and Samantha's. There would be restrictions, however, and Samantha made sure the daycare would be aware of them.

One day, someone had mistakenly given Josh some 'pork-n-beans.' This made Josh break out severely, as he'd had a bad reaction to them. The staff called Samantha at work and she rushed over to the daycare center. It was another thorn. When she arrived and once she laid eyes on him, she didn't recognize him. Both of his eyes were closed shut entirely and his face was swollen so bad that the only way Samantha had recognized him was because of the clothing he'd worn.

Josh was rushed to the hospital and treated. The doctors advised her that if she'd gotten him there five minutes later, Josh would have been dead.

Samantha never returned to the daycare to get his backpack and other belongings. She was frustrated with the daycare, for she'd given them food she'd prepared for Josh to eat.

Shirley Leaper's Home Daycare

Leery of daycares, Samantha had heard about an at-home daycare named 'Shirley Leaper's Home Daycare' from a dear friend. Samantha had gone to check Ms. Shirley out, and while there, she asked plenty of questions. She noticed that Ms. Shirley didn't have a lot of children to care for and that was great and meant she could take care more intently of the children she did have. It was like a one-on-one type of care.

Ms. Shirley was great! Samantha loved her and so did Josh. He'd learned so much from this daycare and Ms. Shirley didn't feed the children fast foods or beans. Ms. Shirley cooked collard greens and sweet potatoes because that was what she'd believed in – home-cooked and wholesome meals. Josh called her Aunt Shirley, and he flourished there.

Gifted Josh

There was a television show called 'Wiggles,' and Josh loved it. There was a 'Wiggles' cartoon show, song, and dance, and Josh knew them all. He knew what time they came on by scrolling down on the TV guide. Sometimes he'd put on his 'Wiggles' pajamas and danced and sung to everything they'd performed. He'd even had a 'Wiggles' car to play with.

Josh could read at the age of three and owned thirty-two children's Bibles. He loved the Word of God. For Christmas, he wanted a Christian store gift card so that he could add more Bibles to his collection. He also wanted for Christmas a Home Depot gift card. He would buy sticks of wood and build crosses for his friends, family, and people in the neighborhood as gifts.

By age five, he knew the Bible very well. He would politely correct people when someone would try to quote Bible scriptures. He never ate candy or sweets other than sweet potatoes. His favorite holiday was Easter. He would put a reef on his head and a white sheet around his body to imitate Jesus. He'd established a post on the computer as he'd taken pictures of himself dressed as Jesus. Each Easter, friends and relatives looked forward to seeing how Josh would dress up like Jesus and how dramatic he would be. It wasn't about the bunny for Josh; it was about the lamb, Jesus Christ.

Josh went to bed reading the Word of God and woke up reading the Word of God. At a young age, Josh knew about the sacrifices of Jesus. He was a great Christian child. He used his sickness not as a way to complain but as an opportunity to thank Jesus for allowing him to get through his agony.

As Josh began to grow, his eczema became worse and it was still painful. He has spent countless nights in the grip of itch, tearing at his skin to wake in the mornings with oozing blisters and gashes on his hands, face, and legs. He'd always say a prayer to the Lord. At times when the chronic itching would be too unbearable, he'd learned to stay calm by meditating on the peace of Jesus Christ. It was this peace that would calm his troubled spirits. He wanted so much to be like a normal child as he'd longed to play outside or go to the mall to shop or to get a simple ice cream cone at the ice cream shop. His quality of life had been compromised and he longed to eat at McDonald's just for the fun of it. Things our children take for granted, Josh only longed for.

Josh Attended School

Samantha and Mike really wanted Josh to attend regular school and be like a normal child, but he just couldn't. They feared of his eczema flare-ups. As time went on, they found a nearby C.E. Galloway School for small children that could handle sick children of many kinds.

Josh finally attended this school, but he was a little skeptical and leery of strangers, as he was taught to watch out by his parents. For months, Josh never spoke a word at this school, not even when asked to. One day, a teacher told him that if he'd wet his pants, he was going to give him some 'act-right medicine,' because he would introduce him to 'Mr. Act Right.'

Of course, Josh told Samantha about the incident on their way home from picking him up from school. Samantha suddenly turned the vehicle around and headed back to the school. Once there, she approached the clerks at the school.

"You all told my baby that you were going to give him some 'act-right medicine' if he'd wet his pants," said Samantha angrily.

"Who told you that, ma'am?" asked a clerk.

"Joshua told me," said Samantha.

"You mean he can talk?" asked the clerk.

"Yes, he can talk. You didn't know he could talk?" asked Samantha. "No, he never said a mumbling word here. We just thought he couldn't talk," said the clerk. "We'll handle the problem, Mrs. Douglas."

"Thank you," said Samantha when she was leaving the school and she was confused why they'd thought Josh couldn't talk.

Samantha returned to the vehicle where Josh was. She had to ask him about the quietness at school.

"Josh, do you talk at school?" she asked.

"No," Josh responded.

"Why not, baby?" asked Samantha.

"You and Daddy told me not to talk to strangers," responded Josh. Samantha was amazed and just didn't know what to say. She and Mike did indeed advise Josh not to talk to strangers, so she tried to define a stranger to Josh so he would understand and know the difference.

Vacation at Hot Springs, Arkansas

Samantha and Mike decided to go to Hot Springs, Arkansas, on their vacation. They'd heard about a mineral-water swimming pool that would be great for Joshua's eczema. The mineral water was good for circulation in the body.

Dianna

'Potassium: eradicates toxins and develops healthy skin

Magnesium: helps to clear complexion and to have healthy-looking skin

Sulfur: aids in respiratory difficulties and skin aggravations

Sodium: lessens inflammation in swollen joints and can aid the lymphatic system

Consistently immersing in a hot spring's bath has been found to minimize eczema soreness, itching, and redness.

Relaxation: Never undervalue the potential of de-stressing and relaxation. A strained state can lead to all kinds of health intricacies, such as depression, high blood pressure, and an enlargement in the output of the stress hormone, cortisol. When Cortisol is disposed in stress-induced measures, this can obstruct our hormonal balance, which in turn adversely impacts just about everything, including our immune system, mood, and our metabolism.

    Circulation: *Particularly sodium bicarbonate and calcium located in mineral hot springs aids good circulation in the body. It can have countless favorable significances, including but not limited to lowering the blood pressure. The encumbrance that comes with defying gravity in the water also aids good circulation.'*

Joshua's bout with eczema had brought him closer and closer to Jesus Christ. Samantha felt that if Joshua hadn't been stricken with severe eczema, he wouldn't have been as close to Christ as he was. It was a good thing that had come out of his disease. He'd always felt that he could win souls for Christ. He'd often quote scriptures and give advice according to God's Word.

While at the mineral pool in Arkansas, Samantha and Mike were relaxing along the sides of the pool and Joshua was in the pool, basking in its coolness. Everything was calm and stress-free. There was an unknown man there on a floater, just relaxing with his eyes closed and enjoying the benefits of the mineral pool.

Joshua noticed that since the man was already laid back in a reclining position and since a lot of water was present, it would be a great opportunity to win his soul for Christ. Joshua suddenly had taken the man and dipped him down under the water, trying to baptize him.

"I baptize you in the name of the Father, the Son, and the Holy Spirit," said Josh. Joshua held the man down as the man was gasping for air and fighting for his life. The man came up confused and surprised and started splashing and gasping for air as he was yelling in *Spanish*.

Samantha and Mike abruptly stopped what they were doing and had gone over to see what was going on with Josh and this unknown man. They wondered what Josh was up to and knew they had to talk to Josh about the endeavor to see why he'd gushed this unknown man under water. They were a little embarrassed but concerned.

"Josh, what are you doing, baby?" asked Samantha.

"I baptized that man, Momma. I saved his soul. See, he was *speaking in tongues*," Josh said. Mike and Samantha were speechless and at a loss for words. They were utterly embarrassed and apologetic to the unknown man.

They knew Josh was a good Christian child but knew they had their work cut out.

That evening, Mike and Samantha decided to talk to Josh about baptizing unknown people. During their conversation, Josh revealed to them that at school one day, there was a gay student walking along the sidewalk. It was a guy walking like a girl. Josh said he really wanted to save this student's soul and didn't want this student to go to hell. So, he baptized the gay student in the sink at school, in the name of the Father, the Son, and the Holy Spirit, that is.

Even today, Josh would have Samantha up till ten p.m. at church services somewhere. Samantha knew that it was important to Josh to be close to Jesus Christ, which had given him so much peace and comfort. She said that she doesn't ever want Josh to feel she won't ever take him to church and doesn't want to be a bad example for him. So, it was church all day Sunday and church on Wednesday and church whenever there was a function going on.

Music

Once Josh had gotten a little older, he had left 'Wiggles' behind and identified very well with music. So, when he saw Michael Jackson for the first time, he was smitten. He knew all of the songs and moves of Michael Jackson. On many occasions, he would imitate him while standing in front of the television.

When it was announced that Michael Jackson had died from an overdose on a drug called 'propofol,' Josh just couldn't understand the reasoning behind the death of the mighty singer. He wondered why Michael Jackson needed propofol when he had everything in life.

One day, when Josh was young, it was time for him to go to the doctor for a checkup. Once in the doctor's office, it was time for a new prescription.

"Don't give me no propofol," said Josh.

"How do you know about propofol, son? I bet you can't even spell it," asked the doctor.

"P.r.o.p.o.f.o.l," said Josh as he correctly spelled the word. The doctor was astounded and somewhat embarrassed at the same time. Samantha just had a smile on her face and didn't say a word.

Home School

Joshua's eczema only got worse the older he'd gotten. The doctors had to give him higher doses of steroids. This only made him sleep all day and awake all night. He did make it up to the second and third grades though. He would sleep during class time and this would not be acceptable at school. So, Samantha was forced to take him out of regular school and 'home-school' her son.

Home-schooling consisted of home bound, which regularly tested the students that were home-schooled. The school agent that had tested Josh for home-schooling wanted to test Josh to see if he was a gifted child because he'd shown how intelligent he was. Once the results returned, it was indeed revealed that Josh was a gifted child.

Josh was really gifted in many courses, but he'd used his experiences in music and acting as a way of relating to different subjects and life itself. Yet, he really desired to be among a group of students at a school setting.

A New Drug in the Market

Commercials on television and the doctors advised Samantha and Mike that there was a new drug on the market called 'Dupixent.' Research has shown this about Dupixent. *'It is used to treat individuals older than twelve years of age that suffer with moderate-to-severe atopic dermatitis, (eczema). It's tropical and is well controlled with prescription therapies used on the skin or who cannot use contemporary therapies. This medication can be used with or without topical corticosteroids. Its safety is not known yet when using on children with atomic dermatitis if they are under the age of twelve.'*

Of course, like other medications, there would be side effects. One of the major side effects was that it retarded reproduction. Now that Josh was sixteen and going on seventeen, Samantha and Mike had a choice to make. Should they immediately stop Joshua's itching and sufferings or take the chance of not having grandchildren or better yet, Josh not living a normal life one day with his own family he'd desired so much.

This drug was a cure for eczema and not a treatment for the problems he'd suffered for so long. Mike and Samantha asked Joshua what he'd wanted. Josh so desired to have a family one day. He wanted a normal family with a wife, children, a house, and a yard. Josh advised that he didn't mind waiting. Since he'd suffered for sixteen to seventeen years already, one more wouldn't hurt. Mike and Samantha decided that since Josh only had a few months to endure the itching and pain, maybe he could endure it a little longer until he was eighteen.

Just the thought that God had given sufferers of eczema a new drug that would *cure* the disease was a great gift from God. Imagining no more itching, pain, sloughing of skin, sleepless nights, and a chance to be normal was indeed a gift from the Almighty God. It was all in God's timing.

There were other experimental drugs that Josh was offered, but Mike and Samantha were against it. They feared more side effects and it would be taking too great a risk. They wanted their child healed but had to weigh the options.

So, Josh had to be eighteen before given Dupixent. My hope is before this book is published, he would be eczema-free, free to live a normal life and free of all the health sufferings he's experienced.

Chapter 24
Family

Mike as a Husband

Marriage brings together two people who love each other. It's about being with someone who makes you happy. The union of wife and husband in body, heart, and, mind is intended by God for their mutual joy, for the help and comfort they give to each other whether in good times or bad. When you've chosen the right mate, it's God's will for procreation of children, the nurturing, and in the knowledge and love of the Lord. The problem can be knowing and not knowing what God's will for a mate is.

Marriage is more than just two people who love each other; it's the foundation for a family. Marriage unites a wife and husband, and marriage unites parents with any children they have and sets the stage for the next generation. What's makes our society strong? A foundation built on strength. Families are the building blocks necessary to form a community and have structure.

Christian marriages benefit our entire society. It allows the couple to raise their children to love and respect God and others. Without Mike in Samantha's life, she explained she wouldn't have known what to do because of the dark pit of thorns she had been in. Mike was an inspiration to her and her soul mate. Their marriage was wonderful, and he was an incredible guy.

Mike loved being near to Samantha, as he'd tenderly shown it. It didn't matter what they were doing together; he just enjoyed being near her. He laughed, made her laugh, made jokes, took her hand, touched her hair, and made her feel like a special woman.

They would oftentimes stay home and watch a romantic movie when Josh was put to bed. They would also go out to eat because he just liked being with Samantha. Their love was adapted into good habits and Josh could tell he was loved because they loved each other so much. If Mike didn't like Italian food, but Samantha did, he would take her to an Italian restaurant just to be near her. She appreciated him and valued the fact that Mike wanted to spend time with her.

Another way that Samantha knew Mike loved her was that he was willing to teach her what he knew and was very patient through the process. He may have felt that in the area of mechanics, Samantha wasn't as smart in the field. That was okay. Mike would take the time to show her things about the mechanics and didn't treat her as though she wasn't a smart person.

Mike was a man that had a great sense of humor and he knew how to make her smile at the right time, especially when she was having a bad day. He would tell her that she'd always made him happy. Samantha may have said something that wasn't really funny, but Mike would crack up just to see her smile.

Being concerned about the family's safety always concerned Mike and he made sure that they were taken care of both physically and emotionally. He wanted to make sure that she and Josh were out of harm's way. Samantha adored that about Mike and she treasured him just the way he was.

Mike could always talk to Samantha about anything from sports to her favorite reality show. He would always listen to what she had to say, as he tried to really understand her. If Mike wanted to talk about his problems, Samantha reciprocated. She always would listen to his problems and respected what he had to say.

When Samantha would, at times, stumble and fall, she could get right back up again, thanks to Mike. He supported her, even when the going got tough. He would always see the good things in her life and was always positive when adversity arrived, as he'd cheered her up when she needed it. It didn't matter how busy he was. He would drop everything for Samantha.

It didn't matter how many great-looking women would pass him by; Samantha was the only woman who owned his heart. He never trusted in another woman's beauty because the Bible said, "Do not lust in your heart after her beauty, or let her captivate you with her eyes." Proverbs 6:25 Mike's commitment to Samantha made her love him all the more.

When Mike would make a mistake, he never denied them, but rather admitted he was wrong and worked to repair the damage he'd done. She, too, would own up to her mistakes and if it seemed to damage the relationship, each would apologize to the other. They did everything they could to understand each other and they admitted to each other their errors.

Mike knew Samantha's favorite color and favorite flower: roses. He'd paid attention to little things of that nature – her likes and dislikes. He truly loved Samantha and was willing to adapt and set aside his own preferences to make things work out.

Putting his ego aside was not a problem for Mike because he loved and respected Samantha. He was always there when Samantha needed him and even when she didn't. He valued her worth and was committed to compromise. He could handle stress without taking it out on his family. Samantha had never had to walk on eggshells around Mike and never had to avoid conflicts because Mike was such an easygoing guy.

Peace Be Still

One day, Samantha was so exhausted by going to work and afterwards from one doctor's office to another. She decided to sit her on her back porch alone and bask in the quietness and stillness of the dusk late evening. Her cellphone was inside, as were Mike and Joshua. At first, she'd planned to just sit for a short moment or two, but in her undistracted stillness, she'd begun to notice things that made her linger just a little while longer.

Samantha had begun to hear the squeaking of the old rocking chair, the buzzing of a bee on the nearby dark pink four o'clock flowers, and the flap of humming bird's wings overhead. The peacefulness of the calm evening had come with the fresh smell of evening air and the sky was brilliantly blue.

Finding herself moved to tears at the response to all God had made, it was the little things she'd never noticed before because her heart was so filled with hustle and bustle, hate, and despair. God, through Mike, had slowed Samantha down long enough to take in the many wonderful creations within her eyesight and earshot that God had created, something she'd never really noticed before.

It was during this time Samantha had realized that God surrounds us with evidence of His glory and tenderness; He made the highest mountains and He also made the branches for the little tiny birds to rest upon. Samantha also realized that God had made her too, and it didn't matter how broken she'd been. He loved her just as much as the tiny little birds and, thus, had given her the perfect helpmate, Mike, to enjoy life with. Knowing what had come before and not what lay ahead, Samantha realized how she should live, and that was one day at a time. Mike taught her that each day is filled with tender mercies from our God and to leave the past behind, only to visit it to help someone.

Mike as a Great Dad

When Samantha first married Mike, she would often wonder what kind of dad he would be. When looking back at her first husband, she now realized that if the five children would have been born instead of the miscarriages, their children would have been in trouble. If this was true, the children would have suffered. She didn't know it for sure, but finding Russell in their bed with another woman would have been a clear indication that their family life was doomed to fail.

Samantha was a little skeptical, at first, getting pregnant for Mike. Yet, unlike the other two husbands, Mike had shown signs of a good husband and she could only hope that Mike would be a good father. As it turned out, she was correct in her analysis this time.

A good father can make all the difference for a child in a family's life. A good father is the pillar of strength, support, and discipline. Oftentimes, his work is thankless and endless. Ultimately, the end result can be shown in the well-adjusted child he'd raised.

A good trait of a great father is that he loves his children and doesn't let them get away with murder. Mike loved Joshua and realized that since he had a skin disease, he would have to discipline him differently. He would let Joshua know when he disapproved of his misdeeds, using tough love to prove a point. Very seldom did Joshua have to be discipline though, but when he did, his father only used words.

On days when Joshua felt better, Mike would even give him chores to do, such as helping with household duties. Mike would never let Joshua take for granted what he and Samantha had. Whether it was the food on the table to a good paid education, Mike made sure that Joshua saw the value in everything they had. This made Joshua understand that his parents were not ATM machines.

Mike was always open-minded and understood that people change over the years and didn't try to maintain the gold standard of his own time. A good example was that Mike understood that couples and families talk more candidly about personal issues than back in the day. Mike knew that it was the breakdown of Samantha's family and was the reason why she'd suffered so as a child. Joshua could talk to his dad about anything, and so could Samantha.

Everyone is different, and Mike knew that too well. He didn't expect Joshua to live the same kind of life he had or do the same kind of work. Mike always respected their values and opinions just as long as they didn't harm the family or anyone else.

Having fun with the family was what Mike enjoyed the most in life. He'd often take the family to games, movies, and would support their favorite sports teams. He would always take time to listen to Joshua and would have a good, easy chat with him. It didn't matter how tired he was. He would always help Joshua with his homework.

Not one time had Mike ever said, 'Do as I say, not as I do.' He would not smoke if he didn't want Joshua to smoke and the same was about drinking. He taught Joshua how to deal with family conflicts, friends, and neighbors by being firm but reasonable on these issues. The way Mike lived was how he wanted Joshua to live.

Mike would illustrate the importance of affection by showing his love for his wife, Samantha, in front of him. They wouldn't argue in Joshua's presence, as he adhered to the values he'd like Joshua to follow. Mike was supportive and loyal to his family.

Lessons were taught by Mike to Joshua from shaving to being courageous because Mike always wanted Joshua to be a well-rounded member of society and not a menace. He taught Joshua proper etiquette, lessons on being honest, and what it meant to keep his word. Most of all, Mike taught Joshua that no matter what, in good times or bad, just be thankful.

Doing whatever he could for his family was definitely Mike. Whether taking a second job to provide for them or just keeping his family out of harm's way, that was Mike. This was instilled in Joshua – the importance of sacrifice. Mike loved his family unconditionally. He provided all the tools he had so that Joshua could become a better person than he was.

I have ten great advices about parenting for dads and being a good husband. I, Dianna the author, only wished that I could have read these tips when I and my husband became a parent.

Dianna

1. **'Don't be concerned about being an extraordinary dad.**

   To be an extraordinary father doesn't mean that you have to have a prerequisite about holding or caressing the baby perfectly. Carefully, not perfectly. It doesn't mean that you must know how to burp your baby instantly or you have to play cowboys and Indians right off the bat. First things first, and that is you have to be a good husband. If you really want to be an extraordinary father, make sure you're an extraordinary husband first, cause extraordinary husbands become extraordinary fathers.

   Raising your child in a stable environment and loving home is paramount. If there's one thing your baby needs, it's an unwavering and loving home. Strive to make your marriage sound and the extraordinary things will shadow.

2. **Start living briskly and allow your wife to have leeway.**

   Burn your candle on both ends, around the side, up the middle, and around the edges before getting married or having a child. Don't do these things when you're married. Be more stable because your marriage and fatherhood will not be able to withstand such lifestyle. Thus, your family life and you will become disgruntled, and it will reach a breaking point and will show sooner or later. However, you and your wife go out every now and then together and on occasion separately. Go out with trusted friend that respect you and your family. This will do the both of you so much good.

   As a father, take your baby out everywhere you used to go before the baby arrived, such as to lunch, breakfast, trips, or shopping. Learn how to do regular things with you baby and you'll soon notice that things will be different. This practice helps parents not to leave their baby in a closed or hot car. It really does help.

   Taking your baby everywhere will cause you to realize that although many things are different now, you can still do a lot of the things you used to do. Go places as a total family and you both will not feel that one or the other has to stay in the house all the time. Get some air time as a family.

3. ***Allow your spouse to have some time alone.*** *Always realize that a father is just as important in a child's life as the mother. Now, a woman has a natural instinct when it comes to caring for an infant. After all, we grew up with baby dolls. Dads, you won't have that instinctive ability from the start. It will be much harder for you at first, but in time you'll get it like a pro. Giving your wife as many breaks as possible is important because she'll need a break. Time to herself is very important to her because she's very focused on making sure the baby has everything they need.*

It will come to a point in time when you'll have to make her take a break. Watching the little one while she naps will be so refreshing to her. Watch the little one when she visits friends or just goes to the mall or sees a movie with friends. It helps tremendously. She needs a break and you need quality time with your little one.

A good father makes sure his wife doesn't get too consumed into being a mother twenty-four-seven.

4. ***At two a.m., get up with your wife to feed.*** *This one, dads, is one of the most difficult part about parenting, other than changing dirty diapers. I think a baby thinks it's a twenty-four-hour night buffet. When they are ready to eat, there's no waiting until the next morning or else, no one gets any sleep, period. And they'll let you know. Help your wife in this area even if you have to work the next morning.*

One morning, my little one continuously woke me up every two hours to eat. I was so exhausted. I just cried. My husband saw the weariness in me and took over for a while. I slept and it seemed like years. The next few days, it happened all over again and my husband helped me the entire time, even though he had to work the next morning.

I showed him the importance of burping and allowed him to burp our little one. He felt great loving on our son. He got to hold his little man once more and cuddled him as well.

Believe it or not, it was great quality time for me and my husband during some of these late-night feedings. We had become closer in our relationship. It was on a different level of closeness than our intimacy could bring. Under the dim lighting, we talked and talked and looked at our son and talked some more. We talked about our beautiful wedding we'd had three years earlier. We even talked about how our parents could have dealt with the difficulties of having a newborn in the house over and over again. It had given us a reason to have greater respect for our parents because we saw how difficult and demanding it was to care for a newborn.

One night, our baby cried and cried to the top of his lungs while kicking his tiny feet. Nothing would appease him and it had awakened my husband. So, my husband took him for a ride in the car at four a.m. I think he had toothpicks in his eyes to keep them open; he was so tired and sleepy. Of course, I took advantage of a good thing. I went straight to sleep. The baby had fallen asleep during the ride and we slept like the three bears.

Just think of moms who had to do it alone numerous times. A woman can respect her husband so much more when he loves and cares for his family. That goes a long way, for it's nothing for me to cook him a gourmet meal with all the trimmings. I love and respect him so much. Such memories of being a wife and new mother, I wouldn't trade the experience for the world.

We've learned through this experience that life is much more than our selfish selves. The sacrifice of raising a child puts self on the back-burner. It makes us more gracious toward others as well.

Treat your children fairly and kindly.

5. **Be warmhearted with your baby, particularly as they get older.** *Children don't understand the word 'love' but they know when it is shown. Telling your baby you love them is meaningless to them but only practice shows it. Words are just that – words. Show them by being a warmhearted and loving father. They can feel a loving touch a mile away. Hugging, snuggling, and kissing them is something that they can relate to immediately. Don't feel awkward about these things. So place your awkwardness on the back-burner and get down to business if you want your child to end up sane in the long run.*

There's power in a dad's touch. By simply hugging them as they walk out the door to school or fixing a loose-end hair twig will go a long way and send signals that you care. Even a simple peck on their forehead is powerful. Remember, if you don't do it, they'll allow someone else to do it and you really don't want that drama.

6. **The way you wanted to be treated as a child is the same you should treat your children.** *Reminisce when you were a child and how you were brought up. Did your dad hug and kiss you? If not, did you only wish that he would? Hug and kiss yours, and don't make the same mistakes your dad did. Break the cycle for the good. Did your dad encourage or criticize you? Did he mold you or left you to fend for yourself? Take the good and change the bad for your children.*

   This is your opportunity to make up for every fatherly injustice your dad did to you by being a much better, diplomatic, and nourishing father. Show your dad that this is how it's done. Dispense your child with a level of forbearance, fondness, love, and understanding that allows your dad to see how it's done.

7. **Don't ever be abusive to your child, ever.** *This golden rule also applies to your wife. Never hit a woman or be abusive to your children. It is a dishonor to all men for a man to hit his wife or child. Only cowards do that. This should be passed on down to your children and should go against everything you're trying to build. Even if domestic violence was present in your family, break the cycle and show the world that you overcame. Domestic violence destroys your family and is the quickest way to a divorce.*

   There is nothing more precious than to see a father, mother, and their children attending their oldest child's graduation together. The dad has his arms lovingly wrapped around his wife and the other children are gleamy-eyed to see their loved one walk across the stage as they cheer them on. It is picturesque and priceless.

   Never berate your wife or child. Never. Don't call them names, period. Make it your objective to give your child so much love and praise, even when they come up short in an area, until they won't have room enough to receive it, and that's a lot.

8. **When getting advice from others, you have to be careful what mentor to follow.** *Regrettably, there is no perfect model on raising children. There*

are thousands of books, of course, on how to be a good parent but even they are contradictory. One may say, "Don't hold your baby when they are asleep," while others say, "Do that for bonding reasons." I found it helpful to ask my mom or grandma many questions and the answers to scenarios. My grandmother had nine children and my mother had five. I figured they were the pros at this.

A lot of information in books and on the internet is good but sometimes wrong. If you think it's wrong, it probably is. There are many questions your pediatrician will be glad to answer. They know babies inside and out. You should listen to that little voice inside your gut and head when answers aren't readily available. That usually keeps you from making bloopers.

Children are little once, so enjoy every minute.

9. **Savor the moment. Life is fleeting.** *Our son is thirty-one now and I can remember when he was seven, eight, and nine years old as though it was only yesterday. One thing about life is for sure; you'll NEVER get those days back no matter what. You can't even buy those days back with all the money in the world. So, enjoy each day and savor each moment you have with them.*

   You should take time off from work every now and then and be with your children. I don't think you'll say on your deathbed, "I wish I'd spent more time at work." You'll say, "I wish I'd spent more time with my child."

10. **Acquire knowledge of what children want most from their father.** *Think about it. Children don't care what kind of job you have, what type of degree you possess, or even how many awards you've earned. All your child wants is to spend time with you. My son, once he'd gotten a little older, loved the fact that I was a police officer. If you ask him what he loves most about me, it's not that I was an officer, but that I was a loving mother. I was a loving mother because I had a loving husband, not one that cursed me out or used me as a punching bag.*

Children want to be near you. They want to hear what your answers to questions will be and they want your truthful and protective answers. They just want to be around their dad as much as possible. They do and will love you unconditionally and forever if you'll let them.'

Mike would dress Joshua's wounds when needed and wipe away his tears when hurting. He would even tear up himself knowing that Joshua wasn't the normal child that could do normal things. Mike's heart would ache at just things of that nature. He'd hoped that one day his son would be able to live a normal life as other children, so careful and pain-free.

Mike as a Loving Father

The birth of first child is a crucial shift in many men's perspective on life. Mike was no exception. From the moment Joshua came home, there was a profound shift to selflessness. In fact, Mike would be quick to admit that with that first glance at his child, he knew immediately that there was nothing he wouldn't do to protect and care for his little person.

Being a father is a role that a man can take on with dignity, predicting the jubilation that comes with watching his children grow up.

Dianna

'A father's love means different things to different people. For some, it is the comfort, reassurance, solace, and encouragement they receive before a big game. For others, it could be the time that dad spent helping with reading homework. But overall, one of the most exceptional things about being a father is that feeling of achievement or attainment when your child, a little person that you fostered, brought up, loved, and taught, does something significant.

For our son, his father's love was one of the most momentous bedrocks of him growing up. Our son loved to do all the things his dad did. Think about that charming image of a father and son fishing or a son handing a wrench to his dad under the hood of a car. No matter what his daddy was doing, you can be certain that our son wanted to do it too.

For a girl, she looks to her dad as an image of what is good and commendable in a man. Dads complement their daughters for their beauty,

190

strength, and intellect, and that in turn strengthens a young woman's impression in herself. A role that young girls appreciate is being daddy's little girl. This is the only exceptional feature that can come from a father. While this role explicitly comes with a remarkable amount of tension, there is nothing more appeasing for a father than having his little girl look up to him.

Equally as important, of course, is a father's love in a young man's life. The father is the one who sets example and a young man learns this only from him. This role should never be taken lightly. A father's chosen career could very well be the one his son will follow. Maybe or maybe not. Many fathers want their sons to have a better employment than themselves, especially in the African-American community. Yet, it is especially exciting when a child attends the same college or university as their dad or takes over the family business. There is no prouder dad than that.

For a father, watching their children grow up is the most important part of his life than seeing his own hair turn grayer. The kisses, hugs, and listening to his child's stories are part of it too, but the amazement of a growing child is priceless. My husband and I still have the wall measurements of our son's growing years, never to be painted over.'

Chapter 25
Major Thorns

Twenty Years of Marriage

You've heard the saying, "If it ain't one thing, it's another." Well, Samantha Douglas broke the mold. It seemed like she was either at the doctor's office for Joshua or Mike due to their illnesses.

After many visits at the doctor's office, it was revealed that Mike needed a pacemaker, an artificial device for stimulating the heart muscle and regulating its contractions. Samantha and Joshua were by his side at all times. Mike did well during the surgery. However, he soon started having complication after the surgery.

Once Mike returned home, started to heal, and was recuperating, he began to have memory loss, for there would be times he would drive places and couldn't remember how to get home. It was gradual at first, but then it had gotten worse over time. They didn't know why this was happening.

Samantha revealed that she constantly had to take Mike to the hospital and no one could ever find out what his problems were. Then, she soon noticed a spot on his foot and by him being a diabetic, time was of the essence. After a battery of tests, Mike had to have his 'metatarsals' taken out. It was the entire bone in his toe.

Mike would be in such pain after surgery that he was given morpheme by the doctors, a high-potent pain pill. He should have been given hydrocodine after surgery, but instead, they'd given him morpheme. He even began to have double vision and Samantha wondered why.

Once given the morpheme, everything began to shut down, for even his heart had stopped. Samantha and Josh were in a panicky state as they themselves, while in the hospital room, hit the code 'blue' button to alert the hospital staff. The staff immediately came and resuscitated Mike from his unconsciousness, but that untimely incident made him very leery of doctors and nurses. So much so, he'd have panic attacks every time one would enter his room. He felt deep down inside that they were trying to kill him, even though they were trying to save him.

Samantha continuously prayed to God that He would intervene on Mike's behalf. The hospital staff sent Mike to a rehab facility with an open wound, furthering his thoughts of doctors and nurses trying to kill him, for the wound should have been closed. Mike was so paranoid and traumatized until it was hard for Samantha to get him to go to his after-checkups at the doctor's office. His paranoia made his heartbeat much faster and that wasn't good at all because it raised his blood pressure.

Taking Mike to every hospital in the town of Shreveport and none being able to pinpoint his illness had become a way of life for Samantha. The doctors just gave him pain pills and one doctor even mistakenly had given him an antibiotic. This caused other problems for Mike and, of course, he had begun to almost hate doctors, but he knew they were lifesavers as well to some point.

As little Joshua would sit by his father's side the entire time, he'd become ill himself in the process with 'impetigo,' a highly contagious bacterial skin infection. It was caused by staphylococcus aureus bacteria. This on top of his eczema really made him sick, uncomfortable, and in a lot of pain.

In and out of doctors' offices and hospital visits were beginning to wear on Samantha. Yet, she found the strength in the Lord Jesus Christ. She prayed:

Samantha

"Lord, the stress I'm experiencing is beginning to take over my life and my family's life. We used to laugh and play games together. Where did we go wrong? Lord, I know that I often lash out at the nurses and doctors when they didn't deserve it. I let my family stress overflow and overcome my thoughts. Lord, help me to manage my stress better so that it doesn't ruin the decisions of the hospital staff for my family. Give them wisdom, Lord. In Jesus's name I pray. Amen."

Months Later

Mike was starting to feel better, until one night Mike started to have flulike symptoms, a fever of one hundred and one, and was sweating profusely. Samantha was up all night, treating his illness. At one time, she wanted to call the ambulance, but Mike vehemently advised against it, and as a matter of fact, he begged her not to call an ambulance even after his temperature had risen to one hundred and five.

After being up all night for aiding Mike's illness, Samantha fell asleep from being exhausted. When she woke, Mike was by her side. It seemed that he was unresponsive. She jumped up and checked his vitals. He had good vital signs and by this time, Josh had awaken. Josh saw all the commotion and panicked after hearing his dad advising Samantha not to call 911. Josh didn't care what his daddy had said. He hurriedly dialed 911.

The medic units arrived and they asked him a series of questions. His vitals were beginning to shut down, so they placed Mike on the gurney as Samantha and Joshua were by his side.

"What is your name, sir?" asked the medic personnel.

"My name is Michael Ellis Douglas, better known as Esquire," Mike replied as he remembered his nickname 'Esquire.'

"Who is that lady over there?" asked the medic personnel, referring to Samantha.

"That's my beautiful wife, Samantha," Mike replied.

"Who is that young man over there?" asked the medic personnel.

"That's my intelligent, God-fearing son, Joshua," Mike replied.

Afterwards, Mike's eyes rolled back in his head as Samantha was listening to those last words Mike spoke. Being in the medical field, Samantha knew all too well that death was nearing. She prayed that this time wouldn't be true for Mike and that God would intervene as He'd done before. Even though Samantha had witnessed it too many times with other patients she'd cared for, she'd refused to believe it was happening to Mike, her loved one. She silently prayed.

Samantha

"Lord, you said in your Word of Psalm 46: 1-2 that you are my refuge and strength, an ever-present help in trouble. ² You are in control. You will

work all things out together for my good. Help my husband, please, Lord. In Jesus's name. Amen."

Unfortunately, on January 18, 2018, Samantha's realizations were true, for Mike passed away. Samantha and Joshua were distraught, to say the least, almost to the point of uncontrollably so. Dealing with the news of Mike's death was one of the most stressful experiences she'd gone through. She felt sick, nauseous, and numb. She felt some unexpected emotions as a result of shock as she'd become out of control. Hospital staff was there to accompany her needs.

Samantha couldn't believe it was happening to the man she'd loved for over twenty years, the one who'd loved her no matter what, the one who'd given her a son, Joshua, the one who'd made her laugh at all times, and the one who'd firmly grabbed her hand and lifted her out of the pit of thorns.

If it weren't for Mike, Samantha would still be living in darkness, she revealed. He changed her life because before Mike, she was always bitter and angry due to her past life experiences. Mike lit her world, as he'd brought her gladness and joy. Mike was such a good person that he would even take the family to church to worship and praise God *every* Sunday because he said the Lord had been so good to them. They were the couple to envy because of their togetherness and fun-lovingness.

Mike taught Samantha how not to live for the past and focus on each day that the Lord had given her. She realized that she could not change the past just like 'spilled milk.' Once it is gone, you can't get it back. If you can't get those days back, leave them there and learn from them, he'd taught her.

Mike learned a lot from Samantha as well. Because of her sexual assaults as a young child, he, too, never let Joshua out of his sight, especially with relatives. He never allowed a male relative to babysit his child, as both did a thorough background check and looked deeper into daycares and schools he'd attended. They asked questions from other parents that attended these schools and talked to trusted staff members, even the janitors, about the school and staff. Samantha and Mike weren't going to allow past experiences to repeat through their one and only child, never.

Home

Returning home from the hospital to the house where Samantha and Mike once shared some of the happiest times in their lives was heartbreaking. The house seemed empty and bland. Mike's belongings were all over the house.

Feeling tired from screaming and crying was an understatement for Samantha. Her muscles ached and sadness, disbelief, and despair overwhelmed her. Relatives began to pour into Samantha's home. Just to have someone to talk to and hug her made all the difference in the world. Neighbors who'd loved Mike also began showing up with tears and stories filled with laughter.

The first night after Mike's death was the hardest for Samantha, even though relatives spent the night with her and Josh. Samantha cried all night, and when she did doze off, she had sweet dreams of her and Mike loving each other as he had a big grin on his face. She'd abruptly awakened to only realize he wasn't there next to her and he was never coming back.

Each day before Mike's funeral was a struggle, but now it was time to make funeral arrangements. Picking out a casket for Mike to lie in was unbearable for Samantha. It was so final. Making sure it was comfortable enough for him to lie in was a part of grieving as though being his caretaker still continued in her spirits. She'd taken care of him for so long, even to the point of being overwhelmed, but pressing on with the help of Jesus Christ gave her strength.

Samantha thanked Jesus for helping her take care of Mike, as well as Joshua, even when she felt like giving up. She realized now that it was all worthwhile and that she'd done everything she could to make sure he'd live another day during his illness. She never complained about working while Mike was at home with his illness. She did what she had to do for the love of her family.

The Funeral

Mike's funeral was huge with friends and relatives. People from all over the country attended. There came ministers from not only the church the family had attended, Shreveport Community Church, a non-denominational church, but ministers from local churches as well. This church had seating of five thousand people and every seat was taken at Mike's funeral.

A special singer flew in from Dallas, Texas, and she sang a breathtaking hymn. The pastor preached on 'fire and brimstone.' Mike never met a stranger and there were individuals there from his pharmacy, Walmart, Isle of Capri, Family Dollar, and even the mail lady was there.

The Golf Cart

It was shared at the funeral that Mike used to drive Joshua around the neighborhood in a golf cart. One day, Mike decided to go to Walmart and he drove into the store aisles. The manager caught up with him.

"Hey, man, you can't ride that golf cart in here," said the manager.

"Why not, man? You have the other electric chairs that people ride in here. What's the difference?" asked Mike. The manager didn't know what to say. They both just laughed and struck up a conversation.

At the end of the funeral, the procession was led by a chariot of horses carrying Mike's body to the grave site. Mike loved horses, and Samantha thought it was befitting for his final ride. She thought if she could get him there on a golf cart, that would be better because Mike loved his golf cart as well, but she couldn't.

Chapter 26
Coping

Grappling

Now that the flowers had faded, the phone calls had ceased, and the food has been eaten up, Samantha and Josh had settled into a new life. Samantha's world had changed due to grappling over the loss of Mike. She had an array of emotions. She felt numb, shocked, and fearful all at the same time. She sometimes would even feel guilty because she was the one who was still alive. At some point, she would feel angry because he'd left her. There was neither a right nor a wrong way to mourn his loss.

Samantha was a trampled rose and it was a struggle putting her life back together. It was difficult for Joshua as he watched his mother be in so much pain. He knew he'd have to be the strong one. He would be hurting inside himself, but he knew his mother was even more hurt by Mike's death than he. Joshua was a great support and Samantha had to learn how to take care of herself while grieving.

Here are ideas for mourners to keep in mind.

Dianna

'Look after yourself. Grief can be hard on your health and wellness. Try to exercise on a regular basis, eat healthy food, and get enough sleep. Try not to start forming bad habits, such as drinking too much alcohol or smoking. This can be an endangerment to your health.

Good Nutrition. Losing interest in eating or even cooking is a cycle of grief for widows. Start eating out with friends or a family member. The fact of eating home alone for a widow can seem detrimental. You can find information on nutrition and cooking in cookbooks or online.

Keep communicating with caring friends. *Allowing family and friends to know when you want to talk about your spouse is very helpful. Some may be grieving too and may salute the chance to contribute to many memories. When others offer you company or help, please accept when necessary.*

Team up with a grief-support group. *It may help sometimes to communicate with people who also are grieving. Conduct research on different outlets such as hospitals, religious communities, and local agencies to find out about support groups. Pick a support group where you feel you fit in, where it is most comfortable to share your feelings and concerns, and which is private. Other members of support groups often have beneficial proposals or know of useful enterprises based on their own involvement. There are some online support groups that make it possible to get help without leaving home.*

Call on members of your church community. *Faith is very rewarding, and many people adhere to it who are grieving. Listening to restoring music, praying, gravitating religious or spiritual texts, or talking with others of your faith also may yield contentment.*

Don't allow yourself to make major changes immediately. *Let some time pass before making huge decisions like changing jobs or moving.*

Consult your physician. *Always continue your regular visits to your healthcare provider. If some time has passed since you've seen your doctor, make an appointment or schedule a checkup. Don't forget to let them know of the changes in your life. If something is taking place in your body, let them know that too and tell them about your everyday activities and if you are having trouble taking care of them.*

Seeking professional help is not to be feared. *Whether it is long-term or short-term counseling, either can help.*

Don't ever forget your children are grieving, too.

When losing a mother or father, the entire family gets hurt dearly and must adjust to the new life without their presence. It takes time. Everything will change but remember that you have your children to care for, and keeping a continual relationship with them is vital. Listen to their feelings and thoughts and be there for them.

Rollercoaster of emotions. *Some days will be remembrances of happy reminiscing while other times, it will be tears and hurting. Each day gets better with time.'*

Today

Samantha spends most of her days now taking care of Josh, for he's her blooming rose. They attend church services on a very regular basis. After all what she's been through, the loss of Mike may have been the worst. She doesn't want to date right now because there are too many thorns out there, but she does miss the feelings of closeness that a *'good'* marriage brings.

At first, it was very difficult for Samantha to cope. It was like losing a limb. She's lost the warmth of physical intimacy and even her own identity. Tears would not be far away, for she's spent countless nights crying for Mike.

Mike was the breadwinner and now she's without funds, plus Joshua needs to be homeschooled again due to his illness. She's trying to find herself again in order to go back to work. "No one will hire you if you're going in ten different directions," said Samantha. She's had setbacks and challenges before, and it was her faith in God that had gotten her through each day then. It will take the same faith at this time too.

A Survivor

Samantha expresses that she was not a victim because victims die in their experiences, whether physically or mentally. A victim is someone who has recently been affected by a bad experience. Samantha said she is a survivor because she's lived through it. A survivor is someone who has maybe gone through a recovery or someone that is discussing the short-term or long-term effects of an incident.

When Samantha looked at herself as a survivor instead of a victim, she has a different take on life. She has ownership over her life and her history. She doesn't let others create life for her, as now she's in control of her choices, good and bad, and she takes responsibility for them.

Transitioning from victim to survivor, Samantha said, wasn't easy. She's entered into the mental health training system as she's taken courses to help not only her herself but others too. She's able to recognize the potential for others in a similar situation as herself. She could recognize when another survivor's story was where she'd still found herself, as they too were traveling the roads of life.

Samantha used to be very resistant to developing coping strategies when dealing with her experiences. She'd oftentimes opted out and just settled for less. It seemed that nothing worked out for her at times and anything she tried was more of a half-arsed attempt than a serious endeavor. She said, "internal powerlessness is the enemy of coping."

Soon, she felt obligated to make an effort. There were others who were dealing with things much worse than the experiences she'd had. Samantha started to recognize each matter she had to deal with and tackled each accordingly. She was able to get a better building strategy on these issues and overcame them.

The most important step for moving from victim to survivor was stepping out of it altogether. Far away for her was being in a better position than she'd ever been because she used to think of herself as a victim of illness. She *never* wanted to be a patient in the mental health institution and fought like heck to stay away.

Even though she hated looking back at the sexual abuse in her life, it was a piece to the puzzle of her life. Her picture wasn't completed yet. Pieces were still yet to be placed.

When Samantha did look back at her life, she couldn't erase it, for that was impossible. It made her feel ill underneath when she'd look back. At times when looking back, to her it would be like quicksand which would have swallowed her up in life had it not been for God and prayers. This could not be for Samantha because she's come too far in life to be taken under from something she had no control over in the first place.

Helping Someone

It can be hard to understand why we suffer. Yet, God can use our affliction in unanticipated ways. As we turn to Him for pleasance and love in the midst of trials, it also empowers us to help others.

Ever blurted out something and didn't know why? Well, Samantha did just that. One day after church, a spirit advised Samantha to go up this unknown gentleman and say,

"You know, I was raped and molested when I was a child," explained Samantha for no apparent reason. The man just stared at her.

"Why would you say that to me?" asked the unknown man.

"I don't know. I felt convicted to say it," explained Samantha. The man had begun to tear up but tried to hide his tears from her. He looked around to see if anyone was listening or looking, to no avail. He began to cry inconsolably. Samantha walked up and gave him a big hug.

"Lady, I've been married for years and I haven't even told my wife that I had been molested as a child by my uncle," the unknown man tearfully explained.

"It's okay, sir. I understand, but you know, it's not your fault, so don't try to hold it in," said Samantha. She wiped his tears away as they chatted a little while longer and then departed as friends.

Samantha

"When I used to go to the doctors' offices for checkups, they often had revealed to me that I had probably been raped since the age of two or three instead of four. I was too young to remember. It is so common in many households, and it needs to stop. I hope that I can get the word out to as many people as I can that this behavior must stop.

My family was against me writing this book in fear of a family embarrassment. I didn't care. The very ones who didn't want me to write this book are the very ones that knew about the rapes and molestations and did nothing to stop it. I really don't care if they are embarrassed. They should be.

I would never allow my child, nieces, nephews, cousins, or even strangers to be subjected to this kind of treatment. The treatment of sexual assault and molestations, I promise to report them to the proper authorities. I can look into a child's eyes and know whether he or she has been molested even through their laughter. I can tell right off and have reported such crimes as soon as I've done my homework.

Long ago, my mother revealed to me that she'd been molested and raped by one of her father's relatives. She said, 'I turned out alright and I thought you could handle it too.'

I told her, 'Mom, you're not alright,' and 'I could not and should not have had to handle it.'"

Dianna

"*Athena, Samantha's mom, was in a nursing home and had been for years. Samantha wants her readers to know that you don't stop loving a parent just because they allowed the abuse. Samantha has always loved her mom but didn't like what she'd allowed to happen to her. Samantha received a phone call from the staff at the nursing home to come there because her mother had fallen ill. When she arrived, she found out that her mother had died from COVID-19. At that moment, Samantha didn't have ill feelings of hatefulness or revengefulness. She kept all of those feelings in the past where they belonged, seldom to resurface. I didn't say never, I said seldom. It has always been Samantha's prayer that her mother would love her like real mothers do. Her prayers were answered in the end of Athens's years. Parents have to be better parents than theirs were. That should be everyone's goal in life. Hate and bitterness destroys.*"

Conclusion

Samantha chooses to be a survivor, a mother, a Christian, a sister, a friend, an artist, a caring person, and a strong person. She accepts being a flawed person and has said she's made plenty of mistakes in life. She's made bad choices on her journey and was rebellious as a child as well. Her identity remains fluid. She is not limited because she's a survivor; she has spurred on to find new understandings, challenges, and new experiences.

Life can be rosy, and as Samantha is just now opening up to live her life, knowing thorns will come her way, she's fearful yet, ready at the same time. She's now in her early fifties, lives for one day at a time, and you know what? It's about time because every day won't be a bunch of roses without their thorns.

CPSIA information can be obtained
at www.ICGtesting.com
Printed in the USA
LVHW010457140521
687424LV00003B/146

9 781645 757412